WHEN
LIFE'S
NOT
WORKING

WHEN LIFE'S NOT WORKING

7 SIMPLE CHOICES
FOR A
BETTER TOMORROW

BOB MERRITT

BakerBooks

a division of Baker Publishing Group
Grand Rapids, Michigan

Published by Baker Books
a division of Baker Publishing Group
P.O. Box 6287, Grand Rapids, MI 49516-6287
www.bakerbooks.com

Printed in the United States of America

Library of Congress Cataloging-in-Publication Data
Merritt, Bob, 1957–
    When life's not working : 7 simple choices for a better tomorrow / Bob
Merritt.
        p.   cm.
    Includes bibliographical references (p.   ).
    ISBN 978-0-8010-1378-2 (cloth)
    1. Discipline—Religious aspects—Christianity. 2. Christian life—Baptist
authors. I. Title.
BV4647.D58M47 2011
241′.4—dc22   2010041209

Published in association with Rosenbaum & Associates Literary Agency, Brentwood, Tennessee.

11   12   13   14   15   16   17   7   6   5   4   3   2   1

For Laurie,
my best friend

Contents

Foreword

Life is difficult for everybody. There are hard jobs, hard marriages, and hard family dynamics. But some people compound their problems by ignoring basic principles that can help them get where they want to go in life.

Where along the way did we forget that discipline is our friend? It's not always going to feel like an ally, but later when you have to rely on a skill you've honed by discipline, you learn that it served you well.

The seven simple choices that Pastor Bob Merritt talks about in *When Life's Not Working* won't make life less difficult, but they may just lead to accomplishment, freedom, and ease. Not *easy* but ease in navigating through life's daily challenges.

Some people really do get from here to there with their lives, marriages, friendships, and jobs intact.

The principles found within *When Life's Not Working* are grounded within the fabric of how God set the world in motion and how he intended for us to live within it.

They also flow out of the life of one of the most adventurous and respected church leaders in the country.

I've known Bob for many years. He is in the top 1 percent of the finest pastors on the planet. He is a man whose mission has always been to see lives transformed by the power of Christ. Even after leading a church from 350 to 13,000, his heart still aches for people who are far from God. When people from Willow are transferred to Minneapolis, we send them Bob's way.

You have someone in your life who needs this book—a son, daughter, parent, or friend. *When Life's Not Working* contains the simple everyday choices that will lead to lifelong freedom and achievement, even for those of us who have made a mess of things along the way. It's never too late to try life God's way, so why not start now.

Bill Hybels
senior pastor, Willow Creek Community Church;
chairman of the board, Willow Creek Association

Acknowledgments

Everything I have comes from the hand of God. And so it's to him that I owe my eternal thanks for pouring the contents of this book into my heart and mind. He is the real author.

And for reasons I'll never understand, God has allowed me to lead an amazing church made up of people who, for the past nineteen years, have put up with my blunders and weaknesses but who still choose to love me.

Eagle Brook is such a part of my identity that I would be lost and grieved without it. I can't thank the people of this church enough for the love and patience that you've shown me for nearly two decades. These have been the most thrilling years of my life.

I am grateful to our board, whose wisdom I cherish and support I need. Thank you for the value you placed on this project by giving me time to write.

To my colleagues on our Leadership Team, your friendship is everything to me. I love the narrative among us that continues to grow, makes us laugh, and makes our team feel like brothers and sisters.

Thanks to agent Bucky Rosenbaum, who picked up my manuscript off a huge pile late one night and saw the possibilities. Thanks to Baker Books, editor Bob Hosack, and all the people at Baker who have made this project so enjoyable. Thanks to George Brushaber for your early edits and encouragement.

My deep gratitude to editor/writer Johanna Price—without your tireless help I would not have been able to finish. And to Jamie, Tahni, Andrea, Jackie, and Katie for your creative touches. Thanks to my assistant Kris Wensmann—you make my life doable.

Sincerest thanks to Scott and Stephanie Sample for availing your getaway on Lake Superior, for stocking your refrigerator, and for cheering me on; also to Harold and Claudia Wiens, Lowell and Bev Rieks, Pat and Debbie Smith, and Steve and Gail Cartier for doing the same.

To my two children, Megan and David—every single day I thank God for the gift that you are to me. I will never understand the depth of God's goodness to your mom and me when he made the four of us a family. You alone have made our lives worth living.

Finally, my deepest devotion and gratitude goes to my best friend for more than thirty-eight years. It's to you, Laur, that I dedicate this book. God has used you to shape my life to become a better man. Thank you for believing in me, challenging me, and sharing your soul with me. I'm still shocked that I got the girl sitting by the window in tenth-grade history class. I know that you're still a little shocked too.

Introduction

Several weeks ago I was sitting under a huge maple tree that canopied over my in-laws' back deck in western Pennsylvania. I needed to go over some notes I'd written, so I put on my glasses, picked up my pen and papers, lifted my feet up on the footstool, and, without warning, the deck chair shattered and instantly collapsed. Have you ever had this happen? You have complete trust, you lean back, and all of a sudden, wham, the bottom drops out.

My arms went flailing, my glasses flew off, I tumbled backward off the deck two steps down, and landed on my butt in their coiled-up garden hose—it all happened in half a second. I had a gash on my right elbow, my thumb hurt, and my left rear was sore. And I didn't bounce right back up and shake it off; I rolled over on my hands and knees, located my glasses, gathered my papers, and then stood to my feet like an overdue pregnant woman.

But now I had a different problem: there used to be four matching deck chairs; now there were three. What do you do when you've completely destroyed your father-in-law's deck chair? Well, you hide it in the garage behind the lawn mower and hope he won't notice until you're gone, which is what I did. When I told my wife about it, she said, "Don't you think he'll notice that they once had four and now they only have three?" "Yes," I said. "But I'm afraid to tell him."

What made it worse is that I have a history of breaking things at my in-laws' house. I broke an end table when I knocked it over rounding a corner; I once broke off a faucet handle while brushing my teeth; and I know I broke his heart when I married his daughter and moved her a thousand miles away to Minnesota. I just didn't want to face the embarrassment and humiliation. So I hid the chair behind the lawnmower and flew home the next day. Two days later when Laurie told her dad what happened he said, "Oh, one of our neighbors broke that chair three weeks ago and I just tried to glue it together. Tell Bob I'm terribly sorry. That chair shouldn't have been out there in the first place."

Nuts. I could've been a stand-up son-in-law, confessed what I'd done, and received all kinds of sympathy. Instead I tried to cover it up and weasel out.

But this is life. Things break, accidents happen, and people make mistakes. Just this morning at the crack of dawn our dog barfed all over our living room floor. I fumbled out of bed, grabbed some cleaner from under the sink, and ended up bleaching the color out of our carpet in three big spots. I never knew that if it's not carpet cleaner, you can ruin your carpet. Now I know.

But deck chairs and carpets can be replaced. It's different when someone's dream collapses, or someone's heart gets broken, or someone's friendship or career gets ruined. But this also is life—things break, accidents happen, and people make mistakes. No one is exempt, and no amount of education, money, or even faith can shield us completely.

But some people are able to regroup and recover from life's losses while others seem to spiral downward. Some people seem to have a deep reservoir of faith, character, goodwill, and healthy relationships that they're able to draw upon when times get tough. It's like having a savings account that gets them through an economic downturn. Economic downturns, just like emotional and relational downturns, are inevitable; those who survive them draw upon the reservoir of strength that they built up when times were good.

Those who struggle the most have little or no reservoir because of choices made along the way that put them in debt, formed addictions, cut short their education, hurt their relationships, and distanced them from God. So when their chair collapses, they have little or nothing from which to draw.

I hear it every week from people who look back on the careless choices they made. "I wish I could go back and relive those years," people will tell me. "Those choices continue to handicap my life."

But the good news is, there is good news. God can, and will, restore us and put us on a new path through his grace and forgiveness. But we have to do our part, which is why I wrote *When Life's Not Working.*

Some people really do have healthy marriages, friendships, and careers, and every one of them has applied the seven simple choices that I've outlined in this book. These choices are woven into the fabric of how God has put the world together, and they're available to every human being—and they're doable.

In part 1 I look at the two options that all of us face in life—the hard life or the harder life. The seven simple choices don't seem simple or easy—and in reality they aren't. But they are *essential* if we hope to prevent a hard life from becoming harder. And because life pretty much comes down to the people in it, part 1 shows why our choices must be fused to relationships.

Part 2 is the stuff of everyday life. Every balanced, grounded, thriving, and joy-filled person I know understands and lives by these seven choices. If life's not working, it's never too late to start on a new path. Let these choices, and God's wisdom, guide your way.

And because none of us get life right all of the time (Romans 3:23 tells us that "all have sinned and fall short"), part 3 is written to bring healing and hope. None of us are beyond the reach of God's love and forgiveness. Part 3 outlines the process of restoration that's available to all of us. I've waited twenty-five years to write about the heart-filled surprises that await the reader in part 3.

Life is hard enough; don't make it harder by ignoring the seven simple choices that God has put before each one of us. If life's not working as well as you had hoped, take charge of your life, get on a different path, and watch how God puts the pieces back together.

PART 1

Foundations for a Great Tomorrow

1

Free Fall

For as long as I can remember, I've wanted to jump out of a plane. I've watched people do it on TV and thought, "Someday I'm going to do that . . ." when I'm older, when I've exceeded my life expectancy, like George Bush Sr., who did his first dive at eighty. When you're eighty, you don't have to worry about your kids' education or your retirement fund; you're good to go. I'm not a big risk taker, and I don't like heights, but when I mentioned it from the pulpit one day, one of my parishioners decided to hold me to it and bought me a $125 ticket for a tandem dive.

Now I was committed.

It's one thing to talk about something like that; it feels completely irresponsible to actually make the reservation and surrender your life to a knapsack at thirteen thousand feet.

The day finally came, and three other guys from our church joined me. We checked our life insurance policies, kissed our wives good-bye, and drove over to Twin Cities Skydive in Baldwin, Wisconsin. It was supposed to be fun, but it felt more like something we just had to get through so we wouldn't be labeled the biggest sissies ever.

After an hour-long training session and signing our names to twenty-five pages of liability release forms, the instructor walked us past the staging area where a bunch of college kids were folding chutes. All four of us stopped, looked at the ragtag group of kids who were barely out of high school, and asked, "How long have you guys been working here?" One kid said a couple years, another said two months, another said a few weeks. So the only thing separating us from life and death was a well-worn chute packed by an inexperienced college kid who was making eight dollars an hour. Not a comforting thought. "Has one of these chutes ever failed?" I wondered out loud. A kid with about eight piercings through his nose and ears responded, "Yeah, but that's why there's a second chute." None of us had the guts to ask if the second chute had ever failed.

By now our nerves were sufficiently shot, but then we met our pilot—Rabbit. Rabbit had a long ponytail and wore a tank top, cutoffs, and no shoes; evidently FAA regulations didn't apply. As he climbed into the cockpit we heard Rabbit say, "I hope I get it right this time."

My friends and I were doing a tandem jump, which means you're strapped to the chest of a "professional." I had Joe, an excitable thirty-year-old with ADD and a love for beer, who said to me before we jumped, "If the chute don't open, the last thing to go through your mind will be my skull." Then he added, "I've only had to use my second emergency chute eight times." Professional skydivers are a rare breed who keep their clients off balance with a mix of sick humor and steely eyed threats, because it's their life too, which is your only source of comfort.

There were nine other jumpers on the plane. We climbed to about ten thousand feet, and suddenly Joe got real serious. He went through the final instructions; double-checked the chute, straps, and altimeter on his wrist; cinched me in tightly to his waist and chest; and said with a loud, stern voice, "Do not pull on anything!" We climbed to thirteen thousand feet. The tension was building. My three friends gave me a nervous look. Then somebody shoved open the door, and it was game on!

The cold air hit us, and we watched the first guy disappear solo out the door and shoot like a bullet toward earth. I felt nauseous. I watched the second guy do the same, then a third. Person after person hurled himself out the door. I thought I might hurl.

My friend Dean and I were the last to go. Dean is a forty-year-old executive at a Minneapolis software company and the father of three young girls. Watching Dean slide toward the door, give a final thumbs up, and fall toward the earth upside down was the freakiest thing I've ever seen. The speed at which he fell made him look like a tiny speck within seconds.

But now it was *my* turn. Joe and I slid toward the door; the wind and the engine noise were deafening. We squatted down. I felt like I was insane, and my mind couldn't process what was happening. But we were warned not to fight it. Skydiving demands 100 percent commitment, so I surrendered myself, leaned forward, and at the count of three, Joe and I jumped.

The first ten seconds were the most intense, most surreal feeling I've ever had. I flipped over headfirst and then was upside down. I felt completely out of control and detached from anything stable. They call it a "free fall," and that's exactly what it is. You're just out there, and the g-force hits your body immediately. Then Joe turned me over, the wind ripped at my face, and I could see the earth coming toward me at 120 mph. We were in a free fall for a full minute, just screaming toward the earth, and you realize that if your chute doesn't open, it'll be over in less than three minutes. I saw Joe check his altimeter, then check it again, and then he hit me on the shoulder, signaling that he was about to pull the rip cord. The critical moment had come. I grabbed my harness and felt a sudden jerk. The chute opened, and we were thrust two hundred feet upward. I realized we were going to live. The rest was an easy glide down.

People have asked me if it was fun and if I'd do it again. It wasn't, and I wouldn't. But I did learn some things: when you're plunging toward the earth with nothing but a backpack and a rip cord, there's no room for error. And you pray that whoever packed your chute did it with precision and that the "professional" on your back didn't go through a bad breakup with his girlfriend the night before. In fact, the most comforting words Joe said to me before we jumped were, "If you touch anything I will punch you in the back of the head. There's only one way to do this or we die." I was genuinely relieved to know that Joe was a "one way only" kind of guy. I learned that Joe was the way, the truth, and the life up there, and it wasn't up for debate. There wasn't a second way or a third way. There was only one way, and Joe was it. I learned that my jump with Joe was his 1,822nd successful jump. Clearly, he'd never had an unsuccessful one, and he made sure of it. I learned that Joe lives by and submits to a proven set of disciplines that ensure his safety every time he jumps. His life depends on it. And there's no deviation, no alternative, no other way. *There's only one way to do this or we die.*

■Life's Disciplines

This is a book on life's disciplines—on self-management, on doing the right stuff in the right order. A life discipline is something you practice over and over again until it becomes ingrained in you, and there's no deviation, because you know that your life depends on it. *There's only one way to do this.* It's different from a principle, which is more theoretical in nature. It's different from a habit, because habits can be good or bad and are often short-lived. A discipline is a behavior, a practice, a way of living that you build into your life so that it becomes a way of life.

God structured the world in such a way that how the world works is predictable and consistent. We don't have to guess about cause and effect because in the Bible God made it clear how he wants us to live and what the natural outcomes will be if we live that way or we don't. He does this out of love. If we choose to live in alignment with how God has structured the world, our lives will work well. But if we live in opposition to how God has structured the world, our lives won't work well and we will end up suffering all kinds of hurtful consequences.

This earth is not heaven, however, and even the most disciplined, most godly people are not immune to illnesses, accidents, and losses associated with a broken, sinful world. A perfectly disciplined life doesn't guarantee a pain-free life. But a person who consistently does the right things in the right order will avoid the unnecessary losses and setbacks that plague those who do the wrong things in the wrong order.

When it comes to skydiving, for example, my friend Joe can count on the consistency of gravity, physics, and wind speed. And if the teenager who packed the chute did it right, Joe will have a safe jump every time. Joe can bet his life on the consistency with which God structured the world, and because of that, he's up to 1,822 jumps and counting.

The same is true for things like marriage, raising children, leading an organization, and staying physically and financially fit. God's ways are consistent for *every* culture and for *all* time. He's given us a set of universal disciplines that are the building blocks to making life work and achieving the best possible outcomes.

A discipline can be learned, but it must be practiced, and it becomes an actual life discipline only when it becomes your natural, automatic response to any and all situations. Disciplines come more naturally to some people than others depending on their upbringing, education, role models, personality, and experience. Today, I am by nature a disciplined person, but it came by watching my father, who was disciplined; he did the right things in the right order, and I reaped the benefits of his consistent life. I never had to guess about his morality, his marriage to my mom, or his commitment to his work or family. I stood on solid ground, and I wanted that for me and my family. These life disciplines work for young and old, male and female, wealthy and poor, religious and nonreligious. Some disciplines are easier to learn and live by than others, and some are counterintuitive, which means they sometimes don't make immediate sense.

The first sentence of Scott Peck's book *The Road Less Traveled* is a timeless truth: "Life is difficult."[1] Life is difficult because it consists of a series of problems that need to be solved. But then he says, "Discipline is the basic set of tools we require to solve life's problems. Without discipline we can solve nothing. With only some discipline we can solve only some problems. With total discipline we can solve all problems."[2]

Peck says that discipline is the key to solving life's problems and that without it we can't solve anything. I think he's dead-on. Living by a set of God-ordained disciplines is the only right way to live and the most liberating way to live. They are the foundational structures in life that produce benefits like achievement instead of failure, reward instead of regret, freedom instead of bondage, intimacy instead of loneliness, wholeness instead of brokenness, financial independence instead of indebtedness. It simply is not possible to achieve personal and professional wellness without living by the principles of discipline that God has put in place for all time and for all occasions. Disciplines are not superimposed punishments. Disciplines are self-imposed *practices* that you apply to yourself willingly, because you have discovered that without them you fail. Peck says, "Without discipline we can solve nothing."

■Two Choices

In Matthew 5–7, Jesus delivered the Sermon on the Mount, which is the essence of what Jesus wanted us to know about life. Boil it all down, and these three chapters contain the most penetrating words in the entire Old and New Testaments. In that sermon, Jesus tackled the most sensitive topics: murder, adultery, divorce, anger, worry, judging others, and the way to salvation. And he didn't sugarcoat them. Matthew recorded, "When Jesus had finished saying these things, the crowds were amazed at his teaching, because he taught as one who had authority, and not as their teachers of the law" (Matt. 7:28–29).

But then Jesus warned his listeners of two roads: "Enter through the narrow gate. For wide is the gate and broad is the road that leads to destruction, and many enter through it. But small is the gate and narrow the road that leads to life, and only a few find it" (Matt. 7:13–14). Jesus says there are two ways to live life. Not one way, not three ways, but two. The choice that every human being has to make is between a broad road and a narrow road, a careless road and a disciplined road. And you can't combine the two. You can't straddle the fence. The Bible says that we have to choose between one of these two roads.

> The Bible says that we have to choose between one of these two roads.

Choice one is the broad road. It's there, and it's available. Jesus describes what the broad road is like: it has no boundaries or restraints, so you don't have to aim at it in order to hit it. It requires no disciplines. It has no list of do's and don'ts, no alarm clocks, no deadlines, no curfews, no responsibilities. It has a broad morality: immorality. It has a broad truth: no truth. And it has a broad freedom, which is actually a false freedom, because it results in breakups, breaches of trust, and bondage.

Many people today suggest that life should not be burdened by disciplines and restrictions. Those things feel constraining, and so they choose the broad road. They also choose the broad road because it is popular. It's not lonely on the broad road. Jesus says that *many* are on this road; you'll have a lot of company if you choose this road because many are traveling it. But Jesus also says that the broad road leads somewhere. Every road has a destination, and the broad road leads to destruction. And he's not just talking about eternal destruction as in an eternal hell someday. He's talking about destruction in all its forms—in relationships, families, careers, and personal health. Jesus says you cannot travel the broad road without its leading to destruction, because there are negative consequences for those who travel this road.

But then Jesus says there's another road, another option, and you and I must intentionally choose to follow it. At first glance, this other road appears to have some disadvantages, because it has restrictions and boundaries. There are certain things you must and must not do. For example, you have to be careful where you walk, how you walk, and with whom you walk, because the Bible says that this is a *narrow* road. You have to aim at it and be careful when you're on it. To quote my skydiving friend, "There's only one way to do this or we die." That's a narrow road. It has restrictions, warnings, and dangers. But some of the best roads I've ever been on were extremely narrow.

A few years ago, my wife, Laurie, and I were on a narrow road in Maui that made us both sweat. I gripped the steering wheel with both hands and heard her say, "Why do I let you talk me into these things?" There were blind curves with rock walls going straight up on one side and five-hundred-foot cliffs that dropped straight down to the sea on the other. And there were no guardrails. I noticed several makeshift shrines with wooden crosses and plastic flowers where people had tragically wandered off the narrow road. But the off-road hikes we took that day led us to cascading waterfalls, magnificent views, and ocean blowholes that are seared into our memory.

So first, this road is narrow, which makes it tough to follow. But Jesus says that what's even more difficult is that "there's only a few who travel it." It can be lonely on the narrow road, and that's hard. When it seems like you're the only one in your school who's trying to live a clean life, that's hard. When you're the only one in your family who goes to church, that's hard. When you're the only one in your work group who doesn't use foul language, that's hard. When you're the only one in your dormitory who's made a commitment to sexual purity, that can be hard and lonely.

But look where the narrow road leads—to life. Jesus says that while the broad road leads to destruction, the narrow road leads to life. And he's not just referring to some distant eternal life in heaven. It is life for the here and now, in all its forms. Jesus says, "I have come that they might have life, and have it to the full" (John 10:10). Jesus wants us to have a full life on earth, filled with family, love, great friends, meaningful careers, financial stability, purposeful contributions to society, and an intimate relationship with God. And all that is possible. Some people really do have "life to the full" in this present life. It's not that they don't have problems or deep losses—nobody's immune to those things—but there's a fullness and joy about them that comes from a life that's well acquainted with the narrow road.

The High Cost of Low Living

Newsweek has a weekly section called *My Turn*, where average people submit a slice of their life for publication. Several years ago I read the story of Judy Edelson, a forty-five-year-old woman who wrote about her experience on the broad road. She titled the article "Not All Bridges Can Be Burned":

> When I was younger, I thought my past didn't mean anything. I thought things left undone, things said in haste, niceties ignored and laws broken weren't important. . . . I used to laugh at my mother telling me, "That will go on your permanent record." I thought I had no permanent record. I was young and had a long, full lifetime in which to make mistakes and explore endless possibilities. I meandered around with drugs,

played the hippie. (I won't tell you how many times I've been married, but it is more than the prerequisite American number of two.) Never was there a moment's concern about the possibility of these events coming back to haunt me later, because there was no later. Just now.

One day I looked around and I was 40. The next day I was 45. I look ahead and I can see 50. Today I have a daughter of my own and I find myself weary of telling her about the dangers of foolish living based on my personal experience. Sometimes I hold my breath when I have to put down a name on a reference list, worrying what that person may know about me. May think about me. May say about me. That comes from foolish living. I used to have the attitude that I didn't care what other people thought about me—it was my life and I was going to live it. . . .

I would like to add some upbeat comment that says, "Oh, well, it was all worth it." But it wasn't worth it. I have so much waste in my past it almost washes away my future. . . . It's like reaching your hand into a big bag knowing there are gems in it but that there's a lot of slimy stuff you would rather not touch. There *is* a permanent record. It lives on in the memories of all the people you've come in contact with. It lives on in your own perceptions of yourself, coloring and flavoring who you become, what you expect to be able to accomplish and how you live your life. . . .

Everywhere I turn my past keeps coming up in polite conversations, job applications and "Mommy, what did you do during the war?" Which is what my precious angel asked me one day. I honestly replied, "Oh honey, I got stoned and missed the war." Then I had to explain to her that I didn't mean people threw rocks at me, but that I lived my life in a slow stupor, wore sandals and see-through shirts, and talked at great length, with utter conviction, about things of which I knew absolutely nothing.

A consequence of foolish living is having to choose my words carefully. Being cautious not to reveal embarrassing elements of my past. Conversations about my college years are restricted to courses of study. Ex-husbands have been transformed into "a friend I used to have" or "an old boyfriend of mine." I don't want my daughter to think that getting married and divorced is no big deal. I don't want her to make the same mistakes and experience the heartache that accompanies an off-the-cuff lifestyle.

So your life history is your permanent record. You can't shake it. You may be able to redeem it with great effort, but given my druthers, I would have written my permanent record with forethought and careful planning, and skipped the would'uvs, could'uvs, and should'uvs. You really can't burn your bridges; they are there even if you change your name and move to a new address. It affects everything you do and hope to become.[3]

Judy admits that she made many poor choices in life that caused personal heartaches and professional setbacks. I think if she could rewind the clock, she'd do things differently. I think she'd think twice about the broad road and give the narrow road serious consideration. I think she'd tell her daughter and the thousands who subscribe to *Newsweek*, "There's a better way to live, so choose wisely; don't wash away your future with a regret-filled past." It's something I wish all young people could learn so that they could avoid the losses that a careless life produces.

One recent evening I was on an exercise machine at a local health club when two high school girls jumped onto the machines next to me and talked with great passion about boys. They took one look at my skinny white legs and black socks and thought, "This guy's harmless, so let's talk." I tried to mind my own business and watch the news, but I couldn't help listening. So I removed my earphones and leaned in. I should probably tell people what I do for a living, but if you're going to have a conversation in public, that's the risk you take—you *could* become sermon material.

One of the girls said that her boyfriend had been two-timing her—she found him drunk with another girl who was also drunk. I leaned in a little farther. She said, "For two weeks, he was doing this, and what's worse is that none of my friends told me about it. I found out who my . . ." and then she used a very bad word, "friends were." I noticed that my heart rate was increasing a little.

They moved on to the topic of which college they were thinking about attending in the fall. One was thinking of a smaller private school but was concerned that maybe she wouldn't be able to find enough parties. The other assured her that if *that* school didn't have enough drinking she could always drift over to parties at the University of Minnesota. I wanted to ask them if their mothers knew about their plans to waste their education on underage drinking and develop a substance abuse habit that could hamper their lives forever.

The conversation shifted to one girl's older brother, who was dating a new girlfriend, but instead of asking how long they'd been dating or what his girlfriend was like, her friend asked, "Are they living together yet?" It just rolled off her tongue as if living together was the next logical step in someone's dating life. At that point I looked down at my machine and noticed that my heart rate was racing off the charts. I also noticed that there was a sadness in my heart and genuine compassion. Historically, I have been hard on people like that, quick to judge, written them off as sinners and losers. I'd at least give them a look, a head shake, maybe even comment on how utterly senseless they were—in a loving sort of way. Those girls were in a free fall headed for a bad ending.

But something happened as I cooled down. I credit the Holy Spirit, who prompted me to close my eyes and pray for those two girls who are eternally loved and valued by God. I prayed for a solid four minutes that God would put his hand on their lives, that he would bring Christian friends into their dormitories and classrooms who would share God's love with them. I prayed that God would one day set them free from a path that could only hurt them. That's our job, by the way. Those of us who are Christians are called to pray for and try to reach those who have lost their way. I believe that God answers those kinds of prayers.

■The Harder Life

Numerous people have said to me over the years, "But, Bob, trying to live a good, Christian life is just too hard." Whenever I hear someone say that, I have to bite my tongue and measure my words, because I could never be convinced, not in a million years, that trying to live a good, moral, Christian life is harder than living a careless, immoral, undisciplined life. The brokenness, loss, and regret associated with a careless, immoral, undisciplined life is far more difficult than the love, joy, and wholeness produced by a godly life. There's nothing easy about living an undisciplined life. There's nothing easy about suffering through multiple partners, addictions, abuse, bondage, and debt.

> There's nothing easy about living an undisciplined life.

At first glance, the principled, moral, Christian life might seem difficult and constrictive, and sometimes it is, but I'll tell you what's harder—coming home to a *third* spouse who can't stand you and kids who don't want to see you, having a boss who won't trust you, and having a bank that wants to foreclose on you all because you were unwilling to follow the ways that God laid out for every human being to follow. I could never be convinced that the good, moral, Christian life is harder than its counterpart. It's not even close.

Bill Hybels said it this way, and twenty years ago when I read this in his book *Who You Are (When No One's Looking)*, I took out my pen and, with heavy hand, underlined every word:

> Some people seem to succeed at everything they try. They have successful careers; they relate well to their families; they may be involved in church and community activities; they are active, growing Christians—they're even physically fit. When

you get close to people like this and try to determine just how they manage to fulfill so much of their potential, you find that in almost every case one quality shows up—discipline.

By contrast, other people have an embarrassing string of setbacks, disasters and failures. If you get close to them, and if they're honest with themselves and you, they'll probably offer you an appraisal of why these calamities have befallen them. "Well, you know, I just started to let things slide," they may say. "I put off doing my homework." "I neglected to follow up leads." "I didn't keep my eye on the store." "I didn't push my chair back from the bar." "I stopped making my calls." "I didn't watch the till." "I didn't take care of myself." "I didn't spend time with my family." "I thought problems would just solve themselves."[4]

I'm telling you, there's nothing easy about a careless life. Nothing. In the words of Judy Edelson, "I thought my past didn't mean anything. I thought things left undone, things said in haste, niceties ignored and laws broken weren't important." Judy learned otherwise, and I applaud her for putting it into print for the whole world to see and learn from. And my guess is that some of you reading these words are saying to yourself, "Bob, you're right. The reason my life is one regret after another is because I lack discipline. I lack stick-to-itiveness. I start something and then I quit. I make poor commitments of time and money that bury me. I cut corners that come back to bite me. I get sucked into bad relationships that hurt me. I'm in a free fall with a bad parachute."

The good news is that there's hope and healing for every human being. Second Corinthians 12:9 says that God's "grace is sufficient." God's grace is sufficient to overcome any sin and put us on a new path. God provided a way for us to be healed and set free from our past failures through the forgiveness that comes when we put our faith in Jesus Christ, who paid for every wrong we've committed with his life, death, and resurrection. It's available to every human being, and it's a gift to be received by faith. But once we receive God's forgiveness, he calls us to lead a different life, a more disciplined life.

How do you get discipline? Where does it come from? A lot of it comes from practicing on a daily basis what Scott Peck calls delayed gratification. Do the hard work first so you can enjoy the results later. Do the hard work first so life will be easier later. It's going to school first so you can get a job later. It's working out first so you can enjoy brownies and ice cream later. It's carrying five credits first so you can have a lighter load later. It's the only right way to live. Henry Cloud says there are only two options in life, either hard/easy or easy/hard: hard first, easy later; easy first, hard later. He says that the only right way to live is to choose hard first so you have easy later.[5]

That's what discipline is all about. It's saving money. It's staying home on Friday night to study for an exam. It's working long hours on a project. It's showing up on time. It's getting up at 5:45 every morning to drive students to school on a two-hour bus route so you can pay for your tuition, which is what some of us did for four years while going to college. It's staying sexually pure and delaying that instant gratification for long-term intimacy in marriage. It's having a goal, rolling up your sleeves, and doing what's necessary to achieve it, believing that all the hard work and sacrifice up front will pay off somewhere down the road. *Because there's only one way to do this.*

■Sucked Under at Dimple Rock

A few summers ago, three dads, a mom, and six of our teenage kids stood near river rafts getting final instructions from a greasy-haired, shirtless, chain-smoking, drifter type about how to navigate the dangerous Youghiogheny River, which cuts through the lower Allegheny Mountains of Pennsylvania. That year, the East Coast was saturated with steady rains, so the river was high and fast. Even the older kids were wide-eyed as the instructor warned us about two spots: Dimple Rock and the Double Hydraulics rapids. Dimple Rock had warning signs leading up to it, urging rafters to exit the river and transport their rafts around it. In huge red letters the signs read: Warning! Dangerous, Life-threatening Rapids. Exit River Here!

Our pre-trip instructor took a long drag on his cigarette and said, "Ignore the signs, but listen up. Choose a captain right now." Two of the dads, Dave and Tim, were chosen as captains and were told to sit in the back of the rafts, rudder them, and bark out orders. The guy waved his cigarette at the rest of us and said without smiling, "This is a dictatorship. Do what the captain says. If he says paddle right, do it; paddle left, do it." Then he told us that to get through Dimple Rock we had to paddle hard and straight leading into it, then, at the captain's command, take a hard left because the rapids want to thrust you into Dimple Rock, flip your raft, and suck you under. Then he said it again, "This is a dictatorship. Obey your captain and you'll make it." We launched, it was wet and wild, and several people got ejected out of our rafts long before Dimple Rock.

About halfway down the river, some of the teens in our raft began to resent our captain, Dave, who took his job very seriously and who, in their opinion, took great delight in bossing us around. They rolled their eyes whenever he demanded, "Remember, this is a dictatorship. You have to do what I say." I heard rumblings of revolt and mutiny, but I'll tell you what, when we came to Dimple Rock, we flew through it like pros. In fact, the kids said, "Was that it?" They were disappointed that it wasn't more eventful. I said, "Believe me, you don't *want* it to be more eventful. People have died here."

Two days later we were sitting in the Pittsburgh airport waiting for our flight home. I picked up a copy of the *Pittsburgh Post-Gazette*, and on the front page I saw the story of a man who had drowned at Dimple Rock the day after we were there. "Andrew Dearden, 46, died Saturday after his raft flipped at Dimple Rock," it reported. "It creates turbulent water that quickly flips a boat and traps a person below the surface, making rescues difficult." I sat there reading in sober silence. "It'll take you down real quick," an expert said of the river. "All five rafters were flipped into the raging surf, four of them surfaced, but Dearden was in trouble and never made it out."

"There's only one way to do this," Joe the skydiver insisted. "This is a dictatorship. Obey your captain," the rafting instructor demanded. We don't like those kinds of words. They feel confining and boring. So we roll our eyes and feel like pushing the captain off the backside of the raft.

But I've learned to respect those words—words like that can keep you alive. And words from our heavenly Captain can keep us alive too: "Enter through the narrow gate," he urged his listeners. "For wide is the gate and broad is the road that leads to destruction, and many enter through it. But small is the gate and narrow the road that leads to life, and only a few find it" (Matt. 7:13–14). Jesus points us to the narrow road because he loves us, because that road leads to life. Be among the few who get on the narrow road, because remember, *there's only one way to do this.*

2

Hog Hole Heaven

I'm a Minnesota boy; it's in my blood. Being in the north woods or along the north shore of Lake Superior is a spiritual experience for me. The aspen, balsam, and jack pine have a wild texture about them, and if I could bottle and sell the fresh smell of the north woods, I'd never have to work again. In the morning, especially, when you first step out of your cabin or tent and breathe in, you instinctively close your eyes and smile because you know you're back.

I'm writing this book at a cabin that sits on the Wisconsin side of Lake Superior, near Bayfield. It has that same smell. The first thing I do every morning is grind the coffee beans, but then I walk out the sliding glass doors and twenty paces to the end of the boardwalk. I look out over Lake Superior, take in a deep breath, and fill my whole being with that wonderful, intoxicating smell of the north. Then after a few hours of writing, I go back out for another hit and I'm good to go for another couple hours. It might sound strange, but that smell touches something deep inside my soul.

There's a remote spot on the Minnesota/Canada border that holds twenty-five years of smells and memories for me, and it's my favorite place on earth. It's a sacred place. If you were to think of your favorite spot in the world, where would it be? Sacred places are important because they recalibrate the emotional and spiritual gauges in our life. They reconnect us with thoughts and feelings that get suppressed by emails and traffic. Sacred places awaken our soul. For Norman and Ethel Thayer, it was Golden Pond. For Noah and Ally in *The Notebook*, it was a backwater passageway that opened up to an aquatic sanctuary. For me, it's a place on Crooked Lake, where every spring I return to catch world-class smallmouth bass and walleyes. The Merritt family calls it the Hog Hole. It's where we catch enormous fish, listen to the wolves howl at night, and watch the northern lights dance across the sky while sitting around a fire. *I* call it Hog Hole Heaven.

It's located in the Boundary Water Canoe Area, so there are no boats or motors—only canoes and an occasional kayak. The Hole itself is no bigger than a tennis court, and if you're even a few feet outside it, you won't catch any fish. It feels like you're in another world when you're there. But there's a price to pay. The road to the Hog Hole is narrow, dangerous, and difficult. *There's only one way to do this*, and it requires that you do the hard work first so you can enjoy the results later. It's the way of discipline.

To get there we leave the Twin Cities at 3:00 a.m., drive four hours straight north to Ely, Minnesota, buy our bait, and then push off at Mudrow Lake. It's a seventeen-mile, eight-hour paddle and portage through a series of lakes and rivers. Once you navigate through the rapids and boulders of the Horse River, you dump into Basswood Lake, where you have to portage your canoes and gear around Basswood Falls. Then it's another six-mile paddle through Crooked Lake, which has a million twists and turns. You come through Bear Paw Pass and around Table Rock and finally into the most remote body of water in the state of Minnesota. The Hog Hole has a deep current running through it, and it's so far back in the wild that only a few locals know about it. One-hundred-fifty-year-old white pines tower over the Hole, glacial rock formations surround it, and at its most narrow point you can throw a stone across from Minnesota to Canada. And at the right time of year, it's loaded with trophy-size walleyes and bass. It's a fisherman's paradise. I'd draw a map for you, but then I'd have to puncture your canoe.

But most people wouldn't want to go even if they knew where it was, because what lies between the Hog Hole and civilization is eight hours of muscle-burning, shoulder-ripping, tongue-hanging, knee-gashing, blister-popping, vein-bursting canoeing and portaging. Getting there isn't easy, which is partly why it's so pristine. It takes a full day of steady paddling and then portaging eighteen-foot canoes and sixty-pound Duluth packs over narrow, rocky paths. Everything you need for a four- to five-day wilderness trip is carried on your back, including food, tents, sleeping bags, cookware, fishing gear, and fourteen dozen minnows and leeches that are sealed in large plastic bags with water and oxygen. It's a narrow road. And it takes enormous effort.

One portage is so brutal that we named it Billy Goat Hill. You have to be a billy goat to get over it. I've seen strong, strapping men collapse halfway up the rocky hill with a canoe over their head and just lay there in exhaustion, unable to get up. But you can't lay there too long because clouds of black flies and mosquitoes swarm to your sweat and blood. And if Billy Goat Hill doesn't get you, swamp portage can bury you in muck. I watched my brother-in-law, Ozzie Larsen, drop down into a muck hole that went up to his knees while carrying two sixty-pound Duluth packs. I was ten paces behind him with the canoe. I trudged passed him and asked, "You all right?" Oz said, "Yeah." We do help each other, but Oz let me know he could manage it, so I kept walking, because everybody knows that you have to carry your own weight. If you twist an ankle or gash a knee, the whole group goes down, because everybody else depends on your ability to carry your load.

So a trip to the Hog Hole isn't for everybody; complainers and freeloaders who don't pull their own weight don't get invited because the trail is hard and unforgiving. And even if they wanted to, most people could never get to the Hog Hole because they lack the disciplines necessary to get there. Most have to settle for overcrowded, overfished metro lakes where they might catch a sunfish or two. I've seen many casualties along the seventeen-mile journey to the Hog Hole—people who didn't plan, were not in shape, brought too much gear, or lost their food packs to bears.

Some people go in and never make it out because they underestimate the undercurrents common to that area. In August 2002, a church group came through Basswood Falls. Two of them went in for a swim but never made it out, even though they were wearing life jackets. The *St. Paul Pioneer Press* wrote:

> The 17-year-old girl and her fellow church campers had been cautious at every step, including carrying their canoes around some of the more treacherous stretches of water. But a break to cool off in what appeared to be a calm stretch of water turned deadly for Jamie Christenson and Eric Hurst, 24, a canoeing guide who tried to save her. Both drowned near Basswood Falls, where a strong current first pulled Christenson under, then Hurst. Both had been wearing life preservers. A third person, an experienced 22-year-old guide who attempted to rescue Christenson, was sucked under, but she survived. "They call these hydraulic currents . . . where the water swirls beneath," said Tim Smalley, boat and water safety specialist.[1]

So why do we do it? Why do we mark our calendars in January, take on a fair amount of risk, and then beat our bodies to near exhaustion to get there? Because once you've been to the Hog Hole, nothing else compares. It's that special.

Some trips are harder than others because of high winds or cold, driving rains. We've flipped a few canoes, lost a few packs to bears, and had our bait stolen by otters, which is bad because we always plan on fish for most of our meals. No bait, no fish. No fish, no food. But every year we return to our piece of heaven—to the smells of the north woods, the taste of fresh coffee brewed over an open fire, and the pole-bending battles with Hog Hole walleye.

One of the realities of life is that few things of value ever come easy. A great marriage takes years of hard work—every day. There is never a time when I can say that I no longer need to work on being patient, tender, and conversant. I believe that marriage is *forever*, which means that you work through your problems and learn how to relate to each other no matter what it takes. Hog Hole marriages require daily effort and sacrifice. So do Hog Hole careers, friendships, children, and churches. It's never easy; few things of value ever are. A Hog Hole life is available to every person, but it takes determination, sacrifice, and work. In a word, discipline.

I'm going to make an assumption that all of us desire to have the best life possible. And when I say *best* life, I mean a life that's marked by what the Bible describes as the fruit of the Spirit: love, joy, peace, patience, kindness, goodness, faithfulness, gentleness, and self-control. The best life is free of addiction, debt, and brokenness. The best life is one that is purposeful and makes a meaningful contribution to society. I'm assuming that you'd rather fish the pristine waters of the Hog Hole than the crowded, overfished lakes where there's one disappointment after another.

You can have that life, but it takes effort. And it all starts with relational wholeness. I'm a disciplined person. I eat right, exercise daily, set firm boundaries, know my strengths, and guard my priorities. I thrive on rhythm and routine and never face a challenge ill-prepared. I live by the adage that "hard work beats talent when talent doesn't work hard." I'm not that talented, so I've had to outwork and out-prepare the competition to be successful. But all of the discipline, fitness, and success in the world is pointless if you end up losing your marriage, kids, or friends.

A Hog Hole life is impossible without first applying life's disciplines to our relationships. It's what Jesus taught his disciples in Luke 11.

■Bring Heaven Down to Our Earth

One day the disciples asked Jesus to teach them how to pray. Jesus said, "This is how you should pray: 'Our Father in heaven, hallowed be your name, your kingdom come. May your will be done on earth as it is in heaven'" (Luke 11:2). Jesus said they should pray for God's kingdom to come to earth, just like it is in heaven.

I wonder how often people pray for God's kingdom to come to earth. Most everyone wants to *go* to heaven someday, but how many of us are praying for heaven to *come* to us? How many of us are hoping to experience some heaven on earth before we die? Jesus says that heaven is not just a future reality; we can start to experience elements of heaven on earth, a Hog Hole Heaven. It's what my seminary professors called "the already but not yet." We have an opportunity to experience some of heaven's forgiveness, grace, joy, peace, and relational wholeness right now, *already*, but on this side of heaven it'll never be complete because we still sin, we still have relational and physical pain, we still have to deal with the process of dying. Heaven's already available, but it'll never be fully complete here on earth. That day when all sorrow, sin, and pain will be gone still awaits us.

Jesus instructed them to pray: God, whatever's going on up in heaven, bring that down to earth; may your kingdom come to earth as it is in heaven. If we can figure out how to bring some heaven to earth, then we'll be fishing in the Hog Hole instead of in some overcrowded, overfished sinkhole.

■A Hog Hole Life

Relationships are the dominant theme of the Bible. Relationships are the essence of life. They are what movies are made of, songs are written about. They are what fuels Facebook, MySpace, and Twitter. Businesses like Kodak, Verizon, and Microsoft have built empires based on relationships.

God is a relational being, and he created us in his image, which means he created us as relational beings. Have you noticed that when your relationships are good, you are good, but when they're bad, almost nothing is good? We are relational to the core; it's how God made us. And the Bible identifies two relationships that are fundamental to a Hog Hole life on earth. In fact, if these two relationships are missing or broken, you cannot experience a Hog Hole marriage, career, family, or life. It's impossible.

What are those two relationships? The Bible says that our relationship with God and our relationships with others are the key to a Hog Hole life; they are the means through which wholeness, joy, and purpose are achieved. So when Jesus said that we should pray for heaven to come to earth, he meant that we should pray for relational wholeness between us and God, and between us and others. When those two areas are in good order, they lead to wholeness in every other area.

When Jesus was asked about the greatest commandment, he said, "Love the Lord your God with all your heart and with all your soul and with all your mind. This is the first and greatest commandment. And the second is like it: Love your neighbor as yourself." Then he said, "All the Law and the Prophets hang on these two commandments" (Matt. 22:37–40). In other words, all the ways that God wants us to live are summed up in these two commands: love God and love others. If we get these two things right, we will be living the way God wants us to live. In fact, love for God and love for others are so closely connected that Jesus links them together. He says the second command is *like* the first. Love for God and love for others are inseparable, and they lead to wholeness in every other area in life.

So if you want to measure how much you love God, look at how much you love, care about, and are considerate of others. If you couldn't care less about other people—if you're not considerate and generous toward others—that's a sign that God's love has not fully penetrated your heart. C. S. Lewis said that we cannot love the whole world, but we certainly can love our neighbors.[2]

It's in the everyday, one-on-one encounters with people that love gets tested. Jesus said, "Whatever's going on up in heaven, bring that down to earth." And what's going on up in heaven, primarily, is love for God and love for others.

> It's in the everyday, one-on-one encounters with people that love gets tested.

By the way, Jesus's instruction to love God and love others in the New Testament is a summation of the Ten Commandments in the Old Testament. The first four commandments address the specifics of loving God: have no other gods before me, don't make false images, don't misuse the Lord's name, and worship God on the Sabbath by keeping it holy. The next six address the specifics of loving others: honor your father and mother, don't murder, don't commit adultery, don't steal, don't give false information about others, and don't covet other people's things. The theme of the entire Old and New Testaments centers on loving God and loving others.

Paul the apostle repeats this theme in Galatians 5:14 when he says, "The entire law is summed up in a single command: 'Love your neighbor as yourself.'" And then he lists the fruit of the Spirit, which is the outcome of a love-filled life: "love, joy, peace, patience, kindness, goodness, faithfulness, gentleness and self-control" (Gal. 5:22–23). These are the qualities that mark a loving person. Then he adds, "Against such things there is no law" (v. 23), which means that if we would treat others with love, joy, peace, patience, kindness, goodness, faithfulness, gentleness, and self-control, there'd be no need for any other commandments because those qualities are the essence of loving God and loving others.

What I've discovered after fifty-three years of life is that when my relationship with God and my relationships with others are healthy, I'm healthy. But when I'm distant from God and when I'm at odds with my wife, kids, colleagues, and friends, I struggle. I go to work and put on a respectable front, but it's with a heavy heart. I try to deal with hard decisions, but I do so with uncertainty and fear. I go golfing or fishing, but it's with loneliness and a lump in my throat.

I have found that when my relational world is out of whack—when I'm not relating closely with God and I'm in conflict with others—then there's not much heaven in *any* part of my earth. Jesus said that we should pray for God's kingdom to come to earth, and that means being in a loving relationship with God and others. It's the foundation to a Hog Hole life. I can be the most disciplined person in the world, I can eat right, work hard, exercise daily, stay focused, and delay gratification, but if my relationships with God and others are missing, I will miss life.

Conviction on the Cranberry River

Some of the best trout fishing in the upper Midwest is near Bayfield, Wisconsin. The Brule River is famous for its large steelhead and brown trout that run in the spring and the fall. Steelies can weigh up to twenty pounds, and when you hook into one, you have to run up and down the stream to try to stay with it.

Early on in my writing, I had come to the end of a long day. It was 5:00 p.m., and I had an unrelenting urge to go trout fishing in a nearby stream called the Cranberry River. The only problem was I didn't have a Wisconsin license. I had arrived late the night before after driving through a bad rainstorm and thick fog. I hadn't seen any bait shops open, and I was just thankful to have made it without hitting a deer. So I had gotten to bed late and then had dove into my writing the next morning. But I had this unshakable hankering to go fishing that evening. It's the same hankering I get every night for vanilla ice cream over a warm brownie with hot chocolate sauce—it's virtually unstoppable.

The stream is less than a mile from where I was staying, but the only place to get a license is eight miles away at the Fish Lips bar in the town of Cornucopia, probably a forty-five-minute round trip. I was planning on going to Cornucopia the next day to get some groceries, and I was going to get my license at the same time. But the urge to go fishing wouldn't go away, and I wanted to get out of the house and get on the stream so badly that I rationalized, "Would the DNR really care if I made a few casts today knowing that they'd get my sixty dollars tomorrow? I just want to get out of the house, make a few casts, and see if the fish are there. What's the harm in that?"

So I suppressed my conscience and drove up Cranberry River Road. I took a right turn toward the river, turned down a dirt road, and there it was, flowing wildly through a valley that was heavily shaded with spruce, birch, and balsam. I was mesmerized. But as I was driving and gazing at the river, I got too close to the ditch, which was muddied by heavy rains, and I sank my Ford Explorer up to the axles. The truck was tilting to one side so badly that I wondered if it might tip. So I shifted into four-wheel drive and tried to back up. The wheels went about a foot and then began to spin. I rocked the Explorer forward and backward, which only sank it farther. I was hopelessly stuck.

It was Saturday evening. I got out of the truck and walked down the dirt road toward a little house. Two big black dogs came running at me barking loudly with their teeth showing. I hesitated, but I had no choice. So I braved the dogs, told them they were nice doggies, walked tenuously up to the one-room, smoke-filled house, and knocked gently. I didn't know if I'd be met with a warm welcome or the barrel of a shotgun.

There was a husband, a wife, and a mother-in-law inside. The man of the house wore a baseball cap, a long ponytail, and cutoffs. His name was Dennis. He had a couple front teeth missing and was watching NASCAR on a forty-inch flat screen TV. Jeff Foxworthy would've had a heyday. When I explained my predicament, the mother-in-law said in a raspy voice, "Good, some excitement." Evidently I was going to be their entertainment for the next hour or so. The mother-in-law looked like she could pull my SUV out with her bare hands. I have a hunting buddy who says, "This is a town where the men are men, and so are the women." She was that kind of woman.

I asked Dennis if he knew of a towing service, and he said, "I have the Toyota truck out there, and if that don't work I have a tractor."

I said, "Really? That'd be awesome." So he backed up to my truck and hooked it up with chains. We slung mud all over the place, but Dennis yanked me out and saved me about a hundred dollars. I said, "Thanks, man. Would you take twenty dollars?"

He grinned and said, "I'm always willin' to take twenty bucks."

Now that should've been enough to convince me to go into town and get my license, but instead I thanked them for their help, opened the back end of my truck, started getting my gear ready to go fishing, and continued to push back my conscience. The three of them were walking back to their house when the mother-in-law stopped, turned around, looked straight at me, and said, "Do you have a fishin' license?"

I was shocked because who does that, and why did she even care? So I said, "Everybody needs a fishing license." And as soon as I said it I thought, "Nice. You're a Christian pastor who just deceived a chain-smoking, NASCAR-watching mother-in-law. How low are you going to go?"

As an aside, one of the ways we love God is by obeying his commands. Deuteronomy 11:1 says, "Love the LORD your God and keep his . . . commands always." That includes being transparent and truthful.

I don't know if it was because I had already sinned plenty that I figured why not sin a little more, or if I was just trying to outrun my conscience. But whatever it was, I dropped down into the stream, stripped some line off my fly rod, and made my first cast, right into a high-hanging tree branch. One cast, one lost fly in a tree. Not to be denied, I got out my cheaters, tied on another fly, made sure there weren't any branches above me, and made a perfect cast, and then another, and another.

I love the sound and feel of a cold trout stream beating against my waders. There's something timeless and native about stepping into a stream that has flowed through the same ravine for hundreds of years. It reminds me of my boyhood when my dad would take me to the Slippery Rock Creek, which cuts its way through the foothills of the Allegheny Mountains in Pennsylvania. One early morning in May, my dad let me skip school, and he dropped me off to fish the Slippery Rock all by myself. It was one of the best mornings of my life. By noon I had caught a limit of eight fat, brown trout on a #2 Meps Spinner. I can still see them swirl out of the current to grab my lure. My dad knew that trout fishing on the Rock is sometimes more important to a boy than sitting in school.

That day on the Cranberry took me back. It was a perfect day, a perfect setting, a perfect stream—*and I didn't enjoy any of it*. After ten minutes of fishing, I lost my second fly in a tree. So how was I doing? So far I'd sunk my truck, lost twenty dollars, deceived a mother-in-law, lost two flies, and caught no fish. I thought, "That's it. I have to make this right."

So I left the stream, drove eight miles to Fish Lips, and handed the lady my credit card. She said, "There's a five-dollar charge if you buy your license with a credit card. So I opened my wallet to pay cash, and I had fifty-seven dollars—three dollars short for the sixty-dollar license. I would have had plenty had I not paid Dennis twenty dollars for pulling me out of the ditch.

So now how was I doing? I'd sunk my truck, lost twenty bucks, deceived a mother-in-law, lost two flies, caught no fish, and paid sixty-five dollars for a sixty-dollar license. Beautiful!

But with my license in hand I drove back to the Cranberry, dropped back down into the stream, and on the very first cast caught a ten-inch brook trout with gorgeous red spots on its side. I stood there all alone in the middle of the stream with shards of sunlight filtering through the trees, and I felt the smile of God again. And I was free. I caught seven more trout after that, and I let each one slip out of my hand and dart back into their hiding places for another day.

When I later phoned my wife and told her about my escapades, she said, "Brilliant. You're writing a book on discipline—it doesn't sound too disciplined to me." Then she said, "You make my whole body hurt." (Laurie has a full-body reaction to my boneheaded missteps.)

What I've noticed is that there's a direct link between loving God and loving others. Whenever I disobey God, it almost always affects other people in a negative way. In this case, by inconveniencing and deceiving complete strangers and causing my wife's whole body to hurt.

I've also noticed that when I'm in the process of disobeying God, I never feel like praying, reading the Bible, going to church, or hearing the truth, because I don't want the truth to get in the way of my disobedience. I don't want to feel God's disapproval or conviction. I don't want to be close to God when I'm intent on disobeying him. Instead, I want to distance myself from him because drawing close to him exposes my sin and shame. I've noticed that disobedience separates me from God, and when I'm distant from God, I'm in a dangerous place. When I'm out of step with God, I become out of step with everyone and everything else, and when that happens, there's not much heaven going on in *any* part of my earth.

Jesus told us to pray for God's kingdom to come to earth, and that can happen only when we are in right relationship with God and right relationship with others. That's the key to a Hog Hole kind of life. So I am slowly learning that if I want more of heaven to come to my earth, I have to keep my relationships with God and others healthy and whole, and the following three directives have helped me do that.

Watch Out for the Little Indiscretions

If I want more of heaven to come down to my earth, it's usually not the big blunders that get in the way—I've been able to avoid most of those. It's the little indiscretions that I try to rationalize away. I've always tried to trivialize the little stuff because compared to the big stuff, what's the big deal? The big deal, I'm learning, is that little stuff often leads to big stuff. And indiscretions are habitual. When I allow myself to cut corners, I'm tempted to do it again and again until it becomes a normal way of behaving that no longer bothers me. The truth is, God isn't concerned about the *size* of disobedience; he's concerned about disobedience.

There was a time when God led Joshua and the Israelites into the Promised Land. Before they crossed the treacherous Jordan River, which was above flood stage, God promised to open a passageway through the river, lead them into Canaan, and drive out the pagan nations they would encounter in battle. God promised them victory at every point as long as they remained obedient. The first people they defeated were the Amorites, who occupied the city of Jericho. God promised victory over the Amorites, but he gave the Israelites a warning before they went in to conquer the city. He said, "Keep away from the devoted things, so that you will not bring about your own destruction by taking any of them. Otherwise you will make the camp of Israel liable to destruction and bring disaster on it. All the silver and gold and the articles of bronze and iron are sacred to the LORD and must go into his treasury" (Josh. 6:18–19). God made it very clear that the devoted things were to be set aside for the corporate good of the nation.

So they went in, the city fell as God had promised, and the Israelites were on their way to overtaking the land that they had dreamed about for forty years. All they had to do was remain obedient in this one small area: *don't touch the devoted things*. But Joshua 7:1 says, "But the Israelites acted unfaithfully in regard to the devoted things; Achan son of Carmi . . . took some of them. So the LORD's anger burned against Israel."

It was just a small indiscretion. What's the harm in siphoning off a few coins from the huge plunder? But God isn't concerned about the *size* of disobedience; he's concerned about disobedience. If they couldn't obey in the little things, how could they obey in the big things? So when Israel tried to overtake the next city of Ai, God removed his hand of protection, and the armies of Israel were soundly defeated.

After the Israelites were defeated, Scripture says that "Joshua tore his clothes and fell facedown to the ground before the ark of the LORD, remaining there till evening" (Josh. 7:6).

But in Joshua 7:10–11, the Lord commands Joshua, "Stand up! What are you doing down on your face? Israel has sinned; they have violated my covenant. . . . They have taken some of the devoted things; they have stolen, they have lied, they have put them with their own possessions." In other words, they had disobeyed in the small things, leading to the defeat of the entire nation. Not much heaven on earth.

Scott Waddle committed an indiscretion nine years ago when he chose to bend the rules and show off his billion-dollar submarine to some guests. It was a momentary indiscretion that destroyed his career and nullified twelve years of training. Scott was captain of the USS *Greenville*, a nuclear submarine. He had graduated at the top of his class and had been handpicked out of 250 naval officers to command this fast-attack sub. His life was a success in every way; he had a great marriage, a beautiful daughter, a bright future.

But then on February 9, 2001, he violated protocol and did an incredible maneuver. In front of his guests, at a high rate of speed, he took his sub from deep ocean waters toward the surface. But just before the sub breached the surface, there was a loud crash. It was one of those moments when you have a full-body reaction. When Scott grabbed the periscope, he saw a Japanese crawler and high school kids scrambling into life rafts. Nine of them died. It became an international crisis, and Scott Waddle was relieved of his command that very day.

Near the end of his book *The Right Thing*, Scott writes these words:

> All of us have those pivotal moments of life when you take your eye off the road and suddenly there's a child on a bicycle right in front of you. Or you allow yourself a momentary indiscretion that has lifelong implications, those seemingly insignificant choices that can suddenly take on a proportion we never dreamed possible. We think, "It could never happen to me," but it did. And in eight minutes my life was totally changed.[3]

At age forty-two, Scott Waddle was able to piece his life back together, but it was at great cost to himself and his family.

I wonder how many of us have allowed ourselves a small, momentary indiscretion that turned out to have lifelong implications. We may think, "Just this once I'll drink and drive. Just this once I'll steal from my company. Just this once I'll have sex before marriage. Just this once I'll cheat on a test. Just this once I'll show off my submarine." As a parent of two teenagers, I found myself repeating things like, "Be careful kids, don't be careless, think about what you're doing and with whom you're doing it, because one bad choice, one small indiscretion can alter your entire life." So watch out for the little indiscretions, because "just this once" can have lifelong implications.

Operate on the Belief That God Rewards Obedience

What it comes down to for me is, do I *really* believe that God exists, that he's involved in my life, and that he rewards obedience and punishes disobedience?

It's a matter of belief.

And my belief gets tested whenever I'm tempted. Belief is easy when I'm not tempted to cross a line, but belief is difficult when the temptation is strong, and I'm all alone, and nobody is looking. But if during the temptation I really believe that God is all-present and all-knowing, and if I really believe that God rewards obedience and punishes disobedience, then there's no question what I should do. So the challenge for me is to operate on the belief that God rewards obedience every time I'm tempted to cut corners, manipulate the truth, or allow myself a little indiscretion. It comes down to belief.

Incidentally, when God punishes, he doesn't cause bad things to happen to people; he simply removes his protective presence. In Joshua 7:12, God said to Joshua, "*I will not be with you* anymore unless you destroy whatever among you is devoted to destruction."

When we are disobedient, it's usually God's protective presence that we forfeit, and that makes us vulnerable to attacks, loss, and failure. God said that the Israelites had made *themselves* liable to destruction. God doesn't have to punish disobedient people directly; he simply has to remove his protective presence, making *them* liable to destruction.

Part of the problem is that sometimes obedience doesn't make mathematical sense. Let's say, for example, that I had decided *not* to buy a license because I was going to fish just that one time. There's a 99.9 percent chance that I could get away with that and avoid paying the sixty-dollar out-of-state license. (My wife frequently comments on how I have a fishing license for every state in the nation.) From a mathematical and human point of view, I would clearly come out ahead.

But what I would have failed to calculate is the God factor. God created the world, he owns the wealth of the world, and if I operate on the belief that God rewards obedience, I will dutifully pay the sixty dollars every time, even for a few minutes of fishing. Maybe God will reward me with the successful publication of a book, a great budget year, or new and fresh insights for my messages. Maybe he will reward me in less obvious ways that I'm not even aware of, like personal health, the protection of my kids, and the well-being of our church and staff.

Or I could disobey and try to cut corners, and maybe God would allow me to slide into a ditch, lose twenty bucks, and end up paying sixty-five dollars for a sixty-dollar license.

In Psalm 119, David writes these words:

> Blessed are they whose ways are blameless,
>   who walk according to the law of the LORD.
> Blessed are they who keep his statutes
>   and seek him with all their heart.
> They do nothing wrong;
>   they walk in his ways.
> You have laid down precepts
>   that are to be fully obeyed. (vv. 1–4)

David says that God has laid down ways, laws, statutes, and precepts, which are different words that mean the same thing; he's talking about God's instructions for life. He says that God has laid down these things for us so that we don't have to guess what God wants us to do or how he wants us to live. He's made it clear, and David says, "They are to be *fully* obeyed."

He also says that those who fully obey God's ways will be blessed. How will we be blessed? He doesn't specify, but we can infer that we will be blessed in various ways—in relationships, health, careers, protection over our family, even financially. Even when it doesn't make mathematical sense, the Bible says that when we do what's right, God rewards us. In Joshua 1:7, God told Joshua, "Be careful to obey all the law my servant Moses gave you; do not turn from it to the right or to the left, that you may be successful wherever you go." It's a matter of belief.

Evaluate the Condition of Your Relationships

I'm a fairly independent, self-reliant person. So I've had to learn how to delegate and let other people do things for me and with me. Sometimes things don't get done exactly the way I think they should get done; sometimes they're done wrong or below standard, and I'm tempted to take them back and do them myself. But one vital lesson the Hog Hole has taught me is that I can't get anywhere alone. I need a team of at least three other guys to make the trip to Hog Hole safe and successful. I need them to help me load the truck, drive at 3:00 a.m., carry sixty-pound Duluth packs, paddle the canoe, cut wood, make fires, filet fish, and clean dishes. And I need them to keep me safe when bears stroll past my nylon tent at night looking for food.

I need people.

I need people to laugh with me, lift with me, and help me achieve things that are beyond me. It's taken me about fifty years to learn that the best part of the Hog Hole is the people with whom I share it. And the best part of my marriage, family, work, and recreation is the people with whom I share those things.

So the Hog Hole life really goes back to loving God and loving people, even for those who've recently lost a job, home, or loved one, or who've gotten rejected by a school, or who can't pay the bills right now. You can overcome if you have a family who loves you, a small group of friends who pray for you, and a God who promises to never leave or forsake you. You will be able to find the strength and resources to overcome any problem if loving God and others is the top priority in your life.

But if you're so out of step with God that he removes his protective presence, and if you're so out of step with others that you find yourself isolated and alone, that's when things tend to spiral downward and living a disciplined life becomes somewhat hollow. It's the "loving God and loving others" part of my life that has allowed me to achieve and excel. The "loving God" part has given me an ongoing flow of wisdom, protection, and strength, and the "loving others" part has given me the tangible love and support to get me through school, build a family, manage a staff, and lead a church. So I have to watch the little things, believe that God rewards obedience, and constantly evaluate the condition of my relationships.

■Hanna's Hugs

Her name is Hanna. She was seven years old at the time and had a mild case of Down Syndrome. I'd seen Hanna on and off for three years because Hanna's brother, Tim, played on my son's soccer team. During those three years, we got to know the other soccer families, and Hanna became a central part of the mix.

But I have to admit that when I first saw Hanna, I felt sorry for her parents and her brother, who sometimes seemed embarrassed by Hanna's bold interruptions. Sometimes she'd wander out onto the field during play, and her parents would have to reel her in. At times she'd walk up to complete strangers and engage them in conversation. And at first I was annoyed by her behavior, but the more I got to know her, the more I began to enjoy her.

Always wanting to be a part of the action, Hanna once wedged her way into the pregame huddle as the boys were getting ready to take the field. Her brother, Tim, gently but firmly nudged her away and said, "Hanna, this is a boys' team," to which Hanna replied emphatically, "I *am* a boy."

Another time Hanna was pacing along the sidelines. One of the parents was admiring her little outfit and said, "Hanna, are you a cheerleader?" Hanna spun around and said with conviction, "I'm the *coach*!" Cheerleader, shmearleader.

But something happened one day that won me over forever. It was the first time I'd seen Hanna in a long time, and I was surprised to see her wearing her own soccer uniform. She was now playing on her own team, and they'd just finished playing at another field. And there was Hanna, working the sidelines as usual, only this time it was different. She started down on one end, and whether she knew you or not, she walked right up to you, got six inches away from your face, and said, "Guess what, I won!" And she said it with such joy and delight that you had to respond, especially when she threw her arms around your neck and hugged you cheek to cheek. One by one, men, women, and children got a "Guess what, I won!" and the most genuine, full-body hug.

I was standing at the end of this procession, and our daughter, Megan, age thirteen at the time, was sitting in a lawn chair dreading her turn. Meg likes her space and isn't much of a hugger, so I knew she was dying inside. Hanna came up to Meg, Meg looked up at me to see if I'd bail her out, but it was too late. Hanna stood about six inches from Meg's face and shouted, "Guess what, I won!" and she threw her arms around Meg's neck. The biggest smile beamed across Megan's face as she embraced Hanna back. *Interesting.*

And then, I couldn't believe it; nobody could. Nobody has ever done what Hanna was about to do in the history of spectator sports. She was about to commit the ultimate soccer sin, the ultimate fan faux pas. Hanna was about to go over and hug the enemy parents who were sitting smugly on the sidelines. I watched with delight as Hanna snuck up on her first victim.

She was a proper-looking lady sitting in a lawn chair, a complete stranger who never saw it coming. Hanna boldly walked up to her, stepped right into her personal space, and said, "Guess what?"

The lady kind of coiled backward and said, "What?"

Hanna threw her arms around the lady, pressed her cheek up against the woman's cheek, and said, "I won!"

What could the lady do? She put her arms around Hanna and said, "That's wonderful."

One by one, men, women, and children—it didn't matter—Hanna stepped right up and gave them each a hug. I noticed that everyone was smiling and laughing because Hanna brought a little bit of heaven to everyone's earth. She sent an electric charge of joy through two opposing teams who now seemed strangely united. And as I watched her, I thought, "Why does it take a little girl with Down Syndrome to do what everyone wants to do but is afraid to do? When do we lose our ability to love boldly and freely, like a child?"

I've often wondered what Jesus meant when he said, "I tell you the truth, anyone who will not receive the kingdom of God like a little child will never enter it" (Mark 10:15). Hanna will probably never be a soccer star, probably never run a business, teach a class, or even have a family of her own someday. Her list of accomplishments won't be long. But she accomplished something on the sidelines that day that nobody else could do or was willing to do: Hanna brought a little heaven to earth, and she showed all of us what Jesus meant when he said, "Love your neighbor as yourself." That's God's kind of love. That's kingdom love. That's how you receive, enter, and experience the kingdom of God on earth, even as it is in heaven.

So you really can have a Hog Hole kind of life, job, marriage, education, career, and soccer team, but it starts with love for God and love for others. It's not easy. It requires enormous effort and sacrifice, but once you've been to the Hog Hole, you'll never want to settle for safe, easy, placid waters again.

It really is that special.

PART 2

Strategies for Intentional Living

3

Give It One More Day

Don't Quit

Firsts are hard. With every "first time" in my life I have wanted to quit. It began on my first day of kindergarten when I missed my mom so badly that I started to cry while sitting at the Play-Doh table. Kindergarten was tough, but if I ever wanted to get to first, second, and third grade, I knew I had to get through it. I've never been thrilled about school—with every first day, first semester, first exam, first report card I have wanted to quit. Now I teach at schools, and I don't know who dreads it more, the students or me.

I wanted to quit my first time at summer Bible camp in fifth grade. Two days into it I was so homesick that the camp director called my parents and said, "In twenty-five years of summer camping, I have never seen someone as homesick as your son. You need to come and get him." When my parents came to take me home, my friend Kent also started crying, so we took him home as well. We were pathetic and proud of it. I never went to camp again.

Toward the end of my senior year in high school, I took a part-time night job at a meatpacking plant. I badly needed a summer job, but when I bear-hugged a quarter side of beef and lifted it off a meat hook, it flattened me right there. It was while lying under a side of beef that I sensed God calling me into church work, so after one shift I quit and painted houses the rest of the summer.

Our first year of marriage was filled with so much tension and conflict that after six months we both concluded we'd married the wrong person. I was in seminary studying to become a pastor, and yet my marriage was falling apart. Whom could I tell? Whom could we go to for help? We were isolated, embarrassed, and thought about quitting. But we just tried to get through one more day, and then another, and then another after that.

I failed so badly in my first preaching class that I thought about walking away from four years of seminary training and becoming a mortician so I wouldn't have to work with people who could talk back to me. I'm dead serious.

And my first year as the senior pastor at Eagle Brook Church was probably the worst year of my entire life. I made all kinds of mistakes, didn't know how to lead a church of 350, and was in deep conflict with several people, including a key staff member. I considered quitting several times during that first year and wondered if I had totally missed God's calling on my life.

It's taken me a long time to learn that every first is hard—first date, first breakup, first day at work, first rejection letter, first baby, first teenager, first major disappointment. When stuff gets hard, it's tempting to quit. And when you're tempted to quit, you sometimes have to hang in there for just one more day.

One of my first major disappointments came when I was a junior in high school. My sophomore year, my lunch table buddies, Mark, Mark, and Daryl each promised me a Hostess Twinkie if I'd join them and go out for the football team. So

I did. I had a great year playing on the junior varsity team as a sophomore, but what really jazzed me was that the tailback for the varsity team was a senior, and it appeared that next year I'd be the starting tailback for the varsity team.

So all summer long my three friends and I worked out, lifted weights, and ran five miles a day. In late August, I entered the two-week football camp as the front-runner for the tailback position.

Summer football camps in the Pittsburgh area are brutal—three to four practices a day, running drills in ninety-degree heat in full pads, stirring up clouds of dirt that stick to your sweat, trying to sleep on bunk beds in a barracks full of high school boys. A hundred guys showed up on the first day, but by day fourteen only thirty-five were left standing. The coaches never had to cut anybody; most of them quit. Any given day there'd be half a dozen guys hanging over the fence throwing up.

But my three friends and I made the varsity squad as juniors, and we were pumped. The *New Castle News* ran its annual predictions, mentioning several seniors and a couple of us juniors as players to watch. But a week before our first game, I was about to face a major disappointment that I never saw coming. Rick was a 170-pound senior with the GQ look. He was lightning fast and had played split end the year before. Rick decided to shift to the tailback position, and suddenly my starting role was in jeopardy.

And I quit. Without telling anyone, I just walked away.

Our coaches couldn't believe it. They'd never had a player survive camp and then quit after making the team. My friends were dumbfounded.

A week later the season started with our first game under the lights, and I sat in the stands huddled next to my girlfriend. Bitter and ashamed, I watched our team take the field. But in the second quarter the unexpected happened.

I watched my three lunch table friends rotate in and out of the game behind some of the starting seniors. And I saw one of them rotate in for Rick! *That would've been me.* And it tore my heart out. I'd been so blinded by my disappointment that I had never thought about the possibility of rotating in and out and sharing the position. I felt sick, and I sat there knowing I should have given football just one more week.

So Monday morning I went to the coach's office, and with humility I asked if there was any way I could get back on the team. Coach wasn't fond of quitters and said he'd have to take a team vote. The vote tipped in my favor, but I would have to pay my dues. Coach relegated me to the junior varsity squad, where I was used mainly as a blocking dummy for the varsity team. You haven't lived until you've seen a 180-pound fullback and a 220-pound lineman running at you like a couple of buffalos—you haven't lived and you might *not* live. I got splattered, spiked, and run over for seven weeks straight, but I endured it day after day hoping it would pay off.

And then it happened. With one game left in the season, Rick went down with a bruised thigh muscle, and everybody wondered who would take his place. I'll never forget walking into the locker room and looking at the information board, where every night before practice the blue *starting* team and the red *practice* team were posted. I looked at the board and just stared. Starting in the tailback position for the final game of the season was *Bob Merritt*. Eight weeks earlier I had been a bitter, defeated person sitting in the stands watching the game. Now I was the starting tailback in the final game against Mohawk High School. The winning team would enter the playoffs.

That rain-soaked Friday night was the biggest night of my life. That night I ran my heart out, punishing and running over defensive backs like I'd been punished and run over for seven weeks. I experienced the incredible high of chewing up yards, smearing my game jersey in mud, and barreling into the end zone for our first touchdown. I felt the backslaps from jubilant teammates and heard the thunderous applause from several thousand fans. And I experienced the agonizing low of fumbling a punt return that contributed to our loss.

I can access that eight-week season in my memory like it happened last week, and I've never forgotten the lessons that have stayed with me for more than thirty years and have helped me push through disappointments and difficult firsts. I learned that often the only difference between those who succeed and those who don't is perseverance. Often it's not intelligence, talent, or strength that wins the day. Those things help, but often it's the person who just hangs in there and outlasts the others for one more day. When you choose to live by the adage "give it one more day," and you push through disappointments and difficult firsts, you have a chance to build a great life. But it's not automatic or easy. You might have to get run over for a while. And that's where we can gain some insights from Moses, who was also tempted to quit.

Moses was born into a Hebrew family but was adopted as a baby into the household of the pharaoh of Egypt during a time when the Hebrews were slaves of the Egyptians. As Moses grew into adulthood, he observed how harshly the Egyptians treated the Hebrews, and Moses ended up killing an Egyptian slave master. When Pharaoh heard of this, he planned to kill Moses, so Moses fled to a desert town called Midian, where he married one of the daughters of Jethro. Moses lived in Midian for forty years, trying to eke out a modest life in relative obscurity. But God had other plans for Moses.

The Bible says that while Moses was tending the flocks of Jethro, an angel of the Lord appeared to Moses in a bush that was on fire but did not burn up. When Moses approached the bush, God spoke to Moses and told him that he'd give him a Twinkie if he'd join the team and lead the Hebrews out of slavery. But when Moses heard God's request, he immediately thought about his deficits and disqualified himself.

People today see the same five deficits and want to quit or disqualify themselves.

■The Inferiority Deficit

God recruited Moses to lead his team, but Moses said, "Who am I, that I should . . . bring the Israelites out of Egypt?" (Exod. 3:11). This is the deficit of inferiority. Inferiority is when you think that everybody else is smarter, stronger, faster, prettier, and better, and you're tempted either to quit the team or not even try. Moses said, "Who am I?"

I wrestle with the inferiority deficit just about every day. I feel inferior to people who are better speakers, writers, leaders, golfers, husbands, and fathers. Why do I feel this way? Because I *am* inferior. There have been and always will be people who are smarter, stronger, and better than me. Every day I'm reminded of how inferior I am. But if I let that deficit determine my life, I will never lead, teach, overcome, or achieve much of anything.

Maybe you've had to battle the question "Who am I?" Who am I to ask her out? Who am I to try out for the team? Who am I to apply for that job? Who am I to go to grad school? Who am I to lead a youth group? Who am I to become a mother or a father? Who am I to leave home and venture out on my own? Everybody feels inferior because everyone has deficits. And even people who end up playing for the team are not without deficits; they just hang in there for one more day, and then one more after that, until their day comes.

Moses said, "Who am I?" Truthfully, he wasn't much. He was abandoned by his parents, rescued from a river, and adopted by a single parent. He committed murder, became a fugitive, and wound up working as an unskilled laborer tending sheep for his father-in-law. Moses had good reason to ask God, "Who am I?" God doesn't deny that Moses has deficits. God simply says, "But I will be with you."

Whenever I feel inferior and ask, "Who am I?" I look up at the plaque that hangs in my office:

I am not, but He is, and He is with me.
I can't, but He can, and He is with me.
I don't want to, but He wants to, and He is with me.
I didn't, but He did, because He was with me.

Moses asked, "Who am I?" And God responded, "You're not much, but I am with you, and that's all you need."

Many years ago I read about an American tourist who was walking through a park in London, not far from Buckingham Palace, and noticed two little girls playing together. Just to make conversation, the tourist asked them who they were, not realizing that they were Princess Elizabeth and Princess Margaret, who were under the watchful eye of their royal attendants. "And who are you two young ladies?" the man asked. One of the royal sisters turned and proudly responded, "Oh, we're nobody, but our father's the king!"

Correction: if your father's the king, you're not nobody; you're somebody! Your life is set. There is nothing you cannot do and nowhere you cannot go. You have instant and direct access to the king and with it all the influence, power, and protection you'll ever need. Princesses Elizabeth and Margaret were too immature to realize that when your father's the king, you have everything.

Moses said, "Who am I?" And God said, "You're nobody, but your Father's the King." And when your Father's the King, you have everything. How many of us live every day with the knowledge that our Father is the King? But it wasn't enough for Moses, so he reminded God of his second deficit.

■The Authority Deficit

In the next verse, Moses said, "Suppose I go to the Israelites and say to them, 'The God of your fathers has sent me to you,' and they ask me, 'What is his name?' Then what shall I tell them?" God said to Moses, "I am who I am. . . . [Tell them,] 'I AM has sent me to you'" (Exod. 3:13–14).

This is the deficit of authority: "On whose authority are you coming to us?"

Moses didn't have the best reputation, even with the Israelites. Sometime after Moses killed an Egyptian slave master, Moses tried to break up a fight between two Hebrews. But one of the Hebrew men questioned his authority: "Who made you ruler and judge over us? Are you thinking of killing me as you killed the Egyptian?" (Exod. 2:14). So when Moses tells God that he has an authority deficit, he's right—he has no authority and no name. So he questions God, "What authority do I have; whose name can I use?" When you lack authority, you sometimes need someone else's authority; you need the backing of someone who is higher up.

When I was fifteen, my best friend, Phil Print, and I skipped school one day. We filled our day with tennis, basketball, and riding our Suzuki dirt bikes up and down the rural roads of western Pennsylvania. It was a great day, until we came speeding over a rise in the road and saw a squad car coming right for us. We both hit the brakes and sprayed gravel everywhere. We were delinquent and under age with no license, no helmet, and no eye protection—all violations of state law. We were in deep deficit.

The officer blocked the road with his car, opened the door, put on his hat, and walked up to us with one hand on his revolver belt. "He's going to shoot us," we thought.

He looked us over and said, "How old are you boys?"

"Almost sixteen, sir."

"Aren't you supposed to be in school?"

"Yes, sir."

"Do you have a license?"

"No, sir."

"Where's your helmet and eye protection?"

"We forgot to wear them."

We thought we were going to jail.

Then he said, "What's your name, son?"

I mumbled, "Bob Merritt."

He got this pensive look on his face and then said with some levity in his voice, "Merritt. You wouldn't happen to be Calvin Merritt's son, the pastor of First Baptist Church?"

I looked at Phil with a glimmer of hope and said, "Yes, that's my dad."

The officer said, "*Really*. I listen to your dad every week on the radio. I *love* your dad. Your dad has changed my life. Would you tell him that Officer Roberts listens to him faithfully and wants to thank him for what he's doing?" And he let us go, a couple of delinquent, law-breaking fugitives.

That day I learned the power and privilege of a name and that when I have an authority deficit, I need to rely on the authority of someone higher up. God told Moses, "I am your authority. Tell them I AM has sent you."

By the way, do you remember Jesus's final words to the disciples in Matthew 28? "All authority in heaven and on earth has been given to me. . . . And surely I will be with you always, to the end of the age" (vv. 18–20). Jesus has all authority over everything and everyone. And he is always with us. When we have an authority deficit, there is a name that is above every name that we can claim as our own. And when we invoke the name of Jesus, we gain access to a power that can pull us through any predicament. But Moses wasn't done listing his deficits.

The Credibility Deficit

The next deficit Moses cited is in Exodus 4:1: "What if they do not believe me or listen to me?" Moses reminds God that he lacks credibility, that he doesn't have the credentials or the track record. "What if they don't believe me?"

So God asked Moses what he held in his hand. It was a staff. When God told him to throw it on the ground, the staff became a snake. When he picked it back up, it became a staff again. God gave Moses the ability to perform miracles

69

in front of Pharaoh so that Pharaoh would know Moses was credible. Moses didn't have any credibility, so God was going to establish Moses's credibility.

Whenever I'm faced with a difficult challenge, I tend to focus on what I *don't* have instead of what I *do* have. I focus on my weaknesses, deficits, and lack of experience and skills—what I *don't* have in my hand. God says, "Stop thinking about what you *don't* have and remember what you *do* have."

What has God put into your hand? For starters, God has given you intellect to think, reason, and create. He's given you strength to work, build, and produce. He's given most of us family, friends, and colleagues who are willing to help us. He's given you the ability to read. (Seventy percent of the world's population cannot read or write. If you can read, you have an immediate socioeconomic advantage over 70 percent of the world's population.) He's given most of us monetary resources that are excessive compared to the world's standards. If you live in the United States and you own a car, you are in the top 2 percent of the world's wealthiest people. Most of us own two or three cars, which puts us in the mega-rich category. He's given us the gift of salvation, forgiveness from sins, and the assurance of heaven when we die. And he gives us an ongoing flow of wisdom and strength, whenever we choose to access it, through Bible study and prayer. Most of us haven't utilized even a fraction of what's in our hand.

For three years I worked on getting my doctorate in speech communication at Penn State University, and for those three years I was a nobody, a number, one of thirty-five thousand students. The speech programs at the Universities of Wisconsin and Minnesota had rejected me, and I was admitted at Penn State provisionally. I had nothing in my hand.

The department administrator was a formidable, single, forty-something woman named Rita. Rita ran the place—even tenured professors flinched in Rita's presence. And if you were a lowly grad student, you were nothing, a bother, an annoyance. I actually liked Rita and enjoyed a tongue-in-cheek banter with her, but if you got in her way, made too many photocopies, or missed a deadline, you were toast. She once slapped my thirty-two-year-old hand and bodychecked me away from the copy machine for not going fast enough. The best I could ever get from Rita was, "What do you want *this* time, Merritt?" She merely tolerated me, a worthless grad student.

The day after I defended my dissertation and was awarded my doctorate, I walked into the main office to make a couple of photocopies, and a miracle happened. Rita got up from her desk, smiled, and with genuine respect and deference said to me, "Dr. Merritt, allow me to make those copies for you. Is there anything else I can do for you?"

I was stunned. I was the same person the day before my defense as I was the day after. I wasn't any more intelligent, gifted, or less bald. I was the same annoying grad student. But now I had something in my hand. And what I had in my hand made me credible in Rita's world. What I had in my hand would open up doors and allow me to teach, write, and lead in areas that otherwise wouldn't have been accessible to me. I'm not an intellectual; it takes me a whole day to write five or six pages for a message or a book. I am very average at every level. But I've tried to take what God has put into my hand and use it to the best of my ability.

> Everybody has a credibility deficit . . . but I would ask you the same question God asked Moses: "What do you have in your hand?"

Everybody has a credibility deficit in some way, but I would ask you the same question God asked Moses: "What do you have in your hand?" Maybe you've come through an addiction, abortion, abuse, miscarriage, or divorce; maybe that's what you have that God can use to help others. I don't have any of those things in my hand, which makes me *less* credible to help those who struggle in those areas. Maybe you have a great marriage, financial stability, or expertise in how to raise healthy kids. God has put something in your hand that he wants you to use to accomplish something great, but he can't do it if you're sitting in the bleachers watching the game.

God put a staff into Moses's hand that would enable Moses to confound Pharaoh, turn the Nile River to blood, and split the Red Sea. Moses had in his hand all the credibility he would need. But he wasn't done complaining about his deficits.

■The Ability Deficit

Moses said to God, "O Lord, I have never been eloquent, neither in the past nor since you have spoken to your servant. I am slow of speech and tongue" (Exod. 4:10).

I find it amusing that the main task God asks Moses to fulfill is in the area of Moses's greatest weakness—speaking. He's like most of us, deathly afraid of speaking in public. (Many people say they have a greater fear of speaking in public than of *death*.)

Add to his fear of speaking the fact that he's bad at it, and Moses has a real deficit. It's not his bag. It'd be like asking me to teach math. This is the ability deficit. Moses said, "I'm slow of speech and tongue." The connotation in Hebrew is that he's got a *fat* tongue. "You're asking me to do something I have never been able to do." Moses isn't exaggerating; it's a legitimate deficit. In fact, he should be commended for being honest about his weaknesses. People associated with *Strengths Finder 2.0* would urge Moses to play to his strengths and not try to be someone he's not. "I can't do it," he says to God.

But this is a key point in understanding how God works in our lives. We typically think of Moses as a superstar leader, handpicked by God to accomplish amazing feats. But Moses wasn't a super anything. Nothing about Moses's upbringing or character was special or extraordinary. And it's not like Moses was excited about God's call on his life. He did everything he could to resist God. Moses was not leadership material. He was, at best, an average human being with several strikes against him.

So why did God pick him? He just did. There is no other reason. God just picked him. He could have picked Aaron, Jethro, or one of the Hebrew slaves. But he picked Moses—*for no good reason.* And God has picked you for no good reason. I believe God wants to take every one of us on an adventure, not because we're super-talented or gifted but because God wants to use us. We've all been around people who are super-talented and bright, and God uses those people in great ways. But this is a story for those of us who are average, nothing special, middle of the pack. That's me. That's probably most of you.

I think too many people miss God's call on their lives and are tempted to disqualify themselves because they look at their lack of ability and think, "There's no way God can use me. I'm not bright enough, talented enough, or strong enough." Or they think they have to wait for their abilities to develop to a high level before they're ready. But God doesn't work that way. *I have never felt ready for anything God has asked me to do.* God doesn't pick us based on our polished abilities; he picks us for no good reason, and then he *supplies* the ability when we follow him. He picks us because he put each of us on earth to accomplish a specific purpose for him. God's purpose for you right now might be to go back to school, raise your kids, support your spouse, teach a class, or mentor those in rehab. Why did he pick you? He just did, for no good reason.

Finally, in Exodus 4:12, God tells Moses, "Now go; I will help you speak and will teach you what to say." The sequence is important. God tells Moses, "Now go." And *then* God says he will equip Moses to do the job. "Get going, and *then* I will help you. Get moving, and *then* I will teach you." God can't teach you anything while you're sitting in the stands watching the game. He works best with a moving target. The question is, are you willing and available to go?

■The Availability Deficit

Moses said, "O Lord, please send someone else to do it" (Exod. 4:13). And this is finally when God got mad. He wasn't angry because Moses did something wrong; he was angry because he did nothing. Nothing upsets God more than someone who wastes their life sitting in the bleachers when they should be on the field. So God reached the end of his patience, relented, and said, "What about your brother Aaron? . . . I know he can speak well" (Exod. 4:14). And God let Moses recruit Aaron to be his spokesperson.

Question: was God going to give Moses the ability to speak and lead? Yes. Was God going to accomplish his purposes? Yes. What it comes down to is being willing and available. God is going to accomplish his purposes—it's just a matter of who's willing and available.

I think Moses missed out. He missed part of the adventure of learning how to speak and lead, and I think it's one of the reasons why God refused to let Moses enter the Promised Land. He gave that privilege to Joshua. God put a call on Moses's life, but Moses told God, "I'm inferior and incapable." And God said, "I know you're incapable. What I want to know is if you're available." If you're available, God will make you capable.

When my son was eleven years old, we took him to an exclusive, private golf course that had a caddie program, and David became a B caddie who was paid eighteen dollars for a five-hour, eighteen-hole loop. We would drive him over at 6:30 a.m., and he'd sit in the caddie house waiting to be called up to carry one of the members' bags—bags that were almost as big as he was and would sometimes drag on the ground. Sometimes he sat all morning and never got called up, and he'd come home dejected. But we encouraged him to hang in there and remain available. When he finally got twenty loops in, he moved up to A caddie, which increased his pay and seniority. The following year he became an honor caddie, and by age fifteen he was a senior caddie earning forty dollars per loop. David simply stayed willing and available.

At age sixteen he got promoted to the bag room, and he started getting spin-off jobs from certain members who began to know and trust him. We told him that the people who get the best jobs and promotions are the ones who are already working. Kids who sit at home during the summer generally don't get promotions. They also don't acquire skills that can take them to a new level.

Then early one spring, right after David turned eighteen, he got a call from the head pro, who asked David to become the full-time caddie master, a job that had been handled by older men. David became the youngest caddie master the Yacht Club has ever had. He was responsible to recruit, train, manage, and pay seventy-five caddies, not because he was any brighter, stronger, or more privileged than anyone else but because he stayed willing and available. And with each promotion, David learned new skills that would take him to the next level.

So are you available? Some people fill their lives with entertainment, travel, golf, acquiring properties, and maintaining an abundance of expensive toys. And they are not available to be used by God in any meaningful or eternal way.

God said to Moses, "I know you're not capable. What I want to know is if you're available. Because if you're available, I will make you capable."

■Encountering Setbacks

So Moses and Aaron finally confront Pharaoh to try to free six hundred thousand Hebrew slaves who've been the workforce for the Egyptians for more than four hundred years. Not a good bet. But in spite of bad odds, God supplies Moses with everything necessary to accomplish the task. He gives Moses supernatural power to do miracles in front of Pharaoh, and he tells Moses exactly what to say. Moses knows that God is leading him. It's a slam dunk!

But when Moses goes to Pharaoh to ask for the release of the Israelites, Pharaoh refuses.

Wait a minute. Didn't God lead Moses and Aaron to Pharaoh? Aren't they following God's plan? Why the opposition? Moses never saw it coming. Maybe they weren't clear, or maybe Pharaoh misunderstood, so they repeat their request: "Let the Israelites go." But Pharaoh retaliates by increasing the work quotas of the Hebrew slaves. When the slaves couldn't keep up, the Bible says they were whipped and beaten. And they blamed Moses for making a bad situation even worse.

What gives? For once in his life, Moses gets a clear leading from God, works through his deficits, finally makes himself available, does exactly what God tells him to do, says exactly what God wants him to say, and things turn ugly. Why? Well, sometimes you have to go through a season when you get splattered, spiked, and run over. Sometimes God needs to take you through some hardships and opposition to prepare you for bigger challenges. And I see four benefits of these kinds of setbacks.

They Build Your Faith

You might be right where God wants you to be, doing what God wants you to do, and still run into obstacles and opposition, often in the form of people who are stronger, faster, smarter, and better looking than you. In my case, it was Rick, the 170-pound, GQ-looking sprinter. For Moses, it was the most powerful person in the ancient world—the pharaoh of Egypt. But God has a way of taking care of pharaohs. You can be right where God wants you, doing what God wants you to do, and still experience incredible opposition. Why? To build your faith.

If Pharaoh had said, "No problem, take the slaves and go," there would've been no turning the Nile River red, no

Red Sea crossing, no pillar of cloud by day and pillar of fire by night, no manna from heaven—and no displays of God's power. Obstacles are opportunities to display God's power. And when we see God heal a bad marriage, turn around an impossible career, remove an addiction, or restore a rebellious teenager, it increases our faith. Setbacks and deficits are opportunities to display God's power and to build our faith.

They Increase Your Strength

In James 1, the Bible says we should actually be joyful whenever we run into problems and trials, because they increase our faith and develop our perseverance. And perseverance leads to strength and maturity. It's not by *avoiding* problems that we gain strength but by going *through* them.

Several months ago Laurie and I sat on a restaurant patio with my daughter and her husband to celebrate Meg's graduation from the University of Minnesota with a degree in educational psychology. It was a beautiful evening. We enjoyed the good food and warm sun and watched Meg open her graduation cards—smiles all around.

Looking at us sitting there you might've thought the past two years were easy. But those two years were filled with daily phone calls from Meg, who said things like, "I hate school; this project is stupid; my teacher singled me out today and embarrassed me. I can't stand her and I want to quit."

Laurie would say to me, "I had to talk Meg off the ledge again today."

Meg would call again and say, "If my teacher calls on me again I'm gonna die" or "This political correctness crap is driving me crazy" or "I'd rather poke my eyes out than go to school. I just want to run away and quit."

She had numerous meltdowns over roommate issues, parking tickets, tuition payments, and more than seven hundred hours of internship work. But there she sat with her master's degree in educational psychology, her license in school counseling, a fistful of graduation cards, and a promising future of job opportunities that she wouldn't have had if she'd given up.

But here's the question: what was happening to Meg every time she made it through a class, internship, tuition payment, or roommate conflict? She gained a little more strength, got a little more confident, gained a few more. skills, and found the courage to take the next step.

What would've happened if she'd given up and quit? She'd be less confident, less knowledgeable, less skillful, and far less prepared for the job market. The Bible says, "Consider it pure joy . . . whenever you face trials of many kinds, because you know that the testing of your faith develops perseverance. Perseverance must finish its work so that you may be mature and complete, not lacking anything" (James 1:2–4).

This verse says that trials play a vital role in our development by making us mature and complete. But most of us try to avoid trials because they're uncomfortable and require effort; they force us to battle through and figure out solutions. But every time you face a problem and you're able to solve it, you get a little stronger. You can't grow without a test; you can't gain knowledge and skills without a challenge; you can't become a person of strength and maturity unless you face difficult trials and learn how to solve them. James says, "Blessed is the person who faces a trial and gets through it, because they will become mature and complete, not lacking in anything" (see James 1).

They Force Us back to God

Moses was called, equipped, and sent by God, but then he ran into resistance and trouble. Exodus 5:22 says, "Moses went back to God" (Message). Don't miss that. Don't rush past that for something more profound: *Moses went right back to God.*

What's the first thing you do when you encounter a severe disappointment or setback? What do you do when you get rejected, replaced, or passed over? Where do you go when you're depressed, broke, confused, or in conflict with people? Do you buy the latest self-help book, run to your therapist, check your horoscope, think happy thoughts, or repeat over and over again, "I'm good enough, smart enough, and dog-gone it, people like me"? Do you first call your mother or your best friend? Moses did none of that. When you're in the pit, there is no gimmick, slogan, or saying that will get you out—sometimes there's not even another person who can help. Sometimes the only thing you can do is go right back to God. And that's what Moses did; it was the *first* thing he did.

How does God respond? In Exodus 6, God repeats the phrase "I will" eight times. I have the "I wills" circled in my Bible. "I will do. I will bring you out. I will free you. I will redeem you. I will take you. I will be your God. I will bring you. I will give it to you." That tells me that God is wiser, more powerful, and more willing than any therapist, book, saying, or person, and he will do for you what you cannot do by yourself, *if you'll just go to him and ask.*

> God is wiser, more powerful, and more willing than any therapist, book, saying, or person, and he will do for you what you cannot do by yourself, if you'll just go to him and ask.

Is there anything you would like God to do for you, free you from, or bring you out of? If so, the next question is, have you actually gone to him in prayer and asked him to do it? It seems like such a simplistic and pointless thing to do; it seems like a weak bailout. But the Bible promises over and over that like a father with his son or daughter, God waits for and responds to his children who come to him in prayer. It's not automatic. God's timing isn't always our timing. Moses still had to go through a season when he got splattered, spiked, and run over by the Red Sea crossing and a surprise attack from the Amalekites. God would honor Moses's prayer, but in God's timing and with the ongoing perseverance and co-operation of his servant. Some people go to God in prayer and expect immediate results, but generally, prayers get answered when people get moving. Prayers get answered when people persevere.

They Teach Us to Push through Quitting Points

Pastor Bill Hybels says that life is full of quitting points, when you have to find the resolve to push through for one more day.[1] I faced a quitting point as a freshman in college. Three days into it I was lonely and afraid and I wanted to go home. Every time I began a new class and received the syllabus, I wanted to quit. Trying to learn Greek was a quitting point. Our first year of marriage was a quitting point. After our son, David, was born, we had two kids in diapers—that was a quitting point. My first year at Eagle Brook I faced a quitting point. Every Monday morning I face a quitting point when I sit down to an empty computer screen and wonder what God wants me to say *this* week that's fresh and life changing.

But here's the question: what kind of person would I be today had I quit school, quit my marriage, quit my church, and quit my job? I'd be an uneducated, unemployed, poor, broken, and lonely person without any experience, wisdom, or future. I'd never know what it's like to score a touchdown, receive a diploma, raise a family, get promoted, be a part of a staff, or lead a church. I'd just be existing. Maybe.

To be human is to want to quit when things get tough. It's much easier to quit a bad marriage than to work through the problems; much easier to quit a team, job, school, church, diet, or exercise program than to work through it. But quitting stunts your growth and stops your progress. It keeps you from building a great life. Now if you're lying under a side of beef or there's some kind of abuse involved, quitting might be advisable. But James 1:12 says, "Blessed is the man who perseveres under trial [blessed are those who push through quitting points], because when he has stood the test, he will receive the crown of life."

I was once picked up by a limo driver in Chicago who was a divorced mother of an eight-year-old girl. She excused her yawn and asked me the standard questions, "How are you today?" "What do you do?" "Where is your destination?" I learned that she'd been divorced for five years after a ten-year marriage. "I don't think he liked having kids," she said. "I haven't seen him since the divorce; he doesn't pay child support." She'd been up since three that morning making runs to and from O'Hare Airport. After driving eight hours, she would go home at noon, lie down for a while, and change into her FedEx uniform, which is her *full-time* job. She would drive from four until midnight for FedEx. "When do you sleep?" I asked.

"I don't get enough sleep—maybe three or four hours a day in between jobs." She drives for FedEx five days a week and the limo seven days a week.

Her daughter, whom she calls her little angel, stays with Grandma. She worries that she doesn't see her enough, but she told me at least three times, "I'll do anything for my little angel—she's everything to me." She hasn't had a vacation in more than ten years and wonders how anyone can afford one anyway. Most of her waking hours are spent driving strangers around Chicago, and when she isn't working, she is sleeping or spending a few moments with her daughter.

This probably wasn't the life she had planned on, but she wasn't giving up. She was pushing through just one more day, then another, then one more after that. She hoped that someday things would be different. I told her that I applauded her for doing everything she could to support herself and her daughter. I racked my brain for something hopeful to say. There was no miracle fix, no easy way out. For now, this was her life, and all she could do was just flat out persevere. I said, "Maybe it will turn for you someday."

"Yeah, maybe in time," she said. "Maybe in time."

I paid my fare, smiled, and said, "There are better days ahead for you. You'll make it." Those words seemed to connect with some place deep inside her. It was the first time I saw her smile.

I don't know what kind of disappointments or deficits you might be facing right now. And your situation might not be what you had planned for your life. But I do know that sometimes all you can do is get through one more day, then another, and another after that, believing that God is teaching you, strengthening you, and doing something in you that will make you more complete. It might take you eight weeks or eight years. But often the only difference between those who succeed and those who don't is flat out perseverance and giving it just one more day.

4

Manage Your Loads

Do a Few Things Well

What did you do today? Take a moment and think about all the things you did today and then ask yourself a second question: is what I did today the way I want to spend my life? Because what you did today *is* your life. Today I spent the first seven hours sitting at our dining room table trying to finish the last few pages of chapter 3. Then I took an hour-long bike ride, ate dinner with my wife, chatted with my kids, read a few chapters from a book, and watched a Meryl Streep movie on TV. That was a good day, because what I did today is how I want to spend my life. What I did today lines up with why God put me on the planet.

Most days I go to the office and spend the day working on a message, interacting with staff, and managing other details. Then I end the day with an hour or two at the gym, followed by a quiet dinner at home with my wife, maybe some reading and flipping between the Twins game and FOX News. Those days also line up with my God-given purpose.

Not every day is like that. On Fridays I golf in the morning and make a big brunch that usually includes blueberry pancakes, bacon, and eggs. Then I take a nap, watch the Golf Channel, hang out with my wife, tinker around the garage or yard, and flip between the Twins game and FOX News. Fridays are when I step off the treadmill and restore. If I am really lucky, my twenty-one-year-old son will join me for a quick pheasant hunt on a nearby farm.

When I asked my wife what she did today and if what she did today is how she wants to spend her life, she said, "I took a walk, read the paper, did the laundry, went grocery shopping, made dinner, talked to the kids, and watched a Meryl Streep movie—yes, what I did today is how I want to spend my life." Call us old-fashioned, but Laurie believes that her twofold purpose on earth is to raise her children and do whatever she can to support me. She's done a great job of creating a home environment that is, as Dr. Phil likes to call it, "a soft place to land." So what did you do today, because what you did today *is* your life.

Now to be fair, everyone has days that seem to have no purpose whatsoever. My most hateful days are when I have to waste two hours going to Home Depot, spend good money on several gallons of deck wash, and then power spray and restain the deck. I tell my wife that it's like taking a marker and putting a big, black X on two days of my life. I always protest that a nice-looking deck isn't worth two days of my life every other year.

So everyone has days that are purposeless, and there can be entire seasons like that. When you're elbow deep in diapers, soccer practices, or paying off school loans, there's not a lot of purpose. When you're a business major sitting in a two-hour geology class, there's not much purpose. Max Lucado says, "Most days are just spent rowing."[1] And that's true. Much of life is mundane—going to work, studying for exams, paying the bills, running errands. Rowing. That's life.

But in between the mundane and routine, how are you spending your life? Have you made any room in your days and weeks for things that really matter and have lasting value?

I ask the question because it's easy to go through twenty, thirty, forty, fifty years of life and keep deluding yourself into thinking that someday you'll finally get around to doing something purposeful. In their bestselling book, *One Month to Live*, Kerry and Chris Shook say it well: "I know so many people whose favorite day of the week is Someday. . . . But when are we going to wake up and realize Someday is today? This is your life, right here, right now. Wherever you're reading this page, feeling whatever you're feeling, facing whatever you're experiencing, *Someday is right now*."[2] That's important because the danger with *someday* is that it can easily turn into *never*. Eventually, you have to look at your life and wrestle with the question of how you want to spend your one and only life. Is what you're spending your life on worth your life?

I think one of the biggest barriers that blocks people from achieving something significant is that they try to do too many things. They lack focus. They don't lack time, because we all have the same amount of time—twenty-four hours each day. If you ask people how they are doing, most will say, "Really busy—I never seem to have enough time." In reality, everybody has the same amount of time; it's how we choose to spend it.

■Narrow Your Focus

A lack of achievement comes from a lack of focus, and a lack of focus comes from trying to do too many things. When people try to do too many things, they end up doing many things poorly and nothing well. Andy Stanley, founding pastor of the twenty-four-thousand-member North Point Community Church in Atlanta, writes, "Devoting yourself to everything, means committing yourself to nothing."[3] People who lack focus haven't thought through the question, is what I did today the way I want to spend my life? And they risk coming to the end of their days having spent their life maintaining all their properties, vehicles, commitments, memberships, and decks. They risk devoting themselves to everything and doing nothing.

When you read about people who accomplish a lot, you find that they all have an ability to focus their energy on one or two things. For example, if you're a biker, you have an appreciation for what Lance Armstrong accomplished by winning the Tour de France a record six times, especially after surviving testicular cancer. The Tour de France is a 2,290-mile road race that's considered the single most grueling sporting event on the planet. But when Lance's testicle swelled to the size of an orange and the cancer metastasized to his lungs, his fight was no longer for the Tour but for his life. He was given only a 3 percent chance to live. Somehow he beat the odds, but weakened by chemotherapy and atrophy, nobody thought he'd ever race again. Even Lance had to decide whether he belonged back on a bike, and he went through a period of severe depression and self-doubt. Lance writes, "I was a bum. I played golf every day, I water-skied, I drank beer, and I lay on the sofa and channel surfed." Eventually Lance had to tell himself, "'I'm alive again, now you need to get back to living.'"[4] Lance decided he needed to refocus his career, so he spent six months training in the Alps and Pyrenees in France. In his book, *It's Not about the Bike*, he writes:

> I only had two things in mind: the Tour de France and having a healthy baby. I geeked out. I did computer calculations that balanced my body weight and my equipment weight with the potential velocity of the bike, trying to find the equation that would get me to the finish line faster than anybody else. I kept careful computer graphs of my training rides, calibrating

the distances, wattages, and thresholds. Even eating became mathematical. I measured my food intake. I kept a small scale in the kitchen and weighed the portions of pasta and bread. Then I calculated my wattages versus my caloric intake, so I knew precisely how much to eat each day and how many calories to burn. My crew called me Mister Millimeter. . . . While I ate breakfast, my wife, Kik, filled my water bottles, and I bolted out the door by 8 A.M. to join Kevin and Tyler for a training ride. Most days I would ride straight through lunch until about 3 P.M. When I came home I'd lie down for a nap until dinnertime. I'd get up again in the evening, weigh my pasta and have dinner with Kik. We didn't do anything. We didn't go anywhere. We just ate, and then went back to bed, so I could get up in the morning and train again. That was our life for six months. Sometimes Kik's friends would say, "Oh, you live in the South of France, how glamorous." They had no idea.[5]

Equally revealing is what Lance and Kik didn't do. They didn't hang out with friends; didn't travel, shop, or recreate; didn't eat pizza, unwind at happy hours, or treat themselves to weekends at the cabin or a vacation at the beach. Winning the Tour was as much about what they didn't do. They ate, slept, and trained for one thing: to win the Tour. And that's the kind of focus it takes to win—at anything.

Most of us will never be world-class racers or have the luxury of riding a bike for a living. But we may have the opportunity to be a world-class student, manager, parent, or leader. And a lot of it depends on focus, on doing a few things well instead of doing many things poorly. So as you think about your life, what do you absolutely want to do well? And what are the activities and commitments that are preventing you from doing it? Because the less you do, the more you will accomplish. If you use the word *someday* a lot, and if you don't want to look back on your life with regret, you need to bring focus into your life. And you can do that by asking yourself five questions.

What Are My Values?

What do you value, and in what order do you value them? Kerry Shook asked a great question: "if your life were to end right now, what would be your biggest regret?"[6] Would it be giving up on school too soon, a job too soon, a marriage or relationship too soon? Would it be a failure to patch up a strained relationship with a parent, child, or friend? If I died today, what would be my biggest regret? More importantly, what should be in my list of highest values so that I can avoid those regrets?

Almost every decision I make—where I go, what I do, whom I spend time with, what I say yes or no to—is based on my five big values. I decided early on that whatever else happened in my life, I wanted to:

1. have a close relationship with God
2. have a great marriage
3. have a strong family
4. be physically fit
5. have a purposeful career

Virtually everything I do, nearly every decision I make, is based on how it will impact my five big values. Why is this so important? Because if you don't know what your values are, you'll just drift, and you'll make decisions based on emotions or emails, and those are bad decision makers. You have to decide what your nonnegotiable values are in life and then devote your time and energy to living accordingly. If you don't know what your values are, you can't possibly follow them.

Let's take the value of being physically fit, for example. Every day after work I come to a stop sign. If I go straight ahead over the bridge, I drive home to a warm house, a warm meal, and a relaxing evening with my wife. If I turn right onto the freeway, I drive ten miles to the gym and endure thirty minutes on the hateful elliptical machine, twenty minutes of dreadful weights, and ten minutes of stretching. Then I shower and get home late. Straight ahead leads to comfort; turning right leads to torture. Every day I face that decision, and five days a week I turn right. Why? Because if I keep going straight, I can't achieve my goals. As hard as it is to turn right, the payoff is worth it. I'm stronger and healthier, I have more energy, and I'm in a better mood when I get home. But it's the value that drives my decision and determines where I go and what I do; it narrows my focus and eliminates competing options. Where might you need to take a right this week, this month, this year? You won't know unless you've established your values.

My second top value is to have a great marriage. I knew that a great marriage would impact every other value. I didn't just want to get married; anybody can get married. I wanted a lifelong marriage filled with intimacy, friendship, memories, and security. That value drove my decision to stay sexually pure all through my teen years and early twenties. I wanted to bring my sexual purity to my marriage because it's difficult to build a great marriage with a sexual past that's been compromised over and over again. The Bible says that when a couple comes together sexually, they become "one flesh," which means that there's not just a physical union but also a spiritual union. But when that oneness is severed by having multiple sexual partners, there's a tearing of the soul that makes intimacy in marriage difficult to achieve. It's why Jesus says, "What God has brought together, let nobody separate" (Matt. 19:6, author paraphrase).

There is forgiveness available for those who have failed in this area, but the damage that comes from exploiting the most personal and private part of who a person is can be very difficult to overcome. So the value of having a great marriage drove my decisions to stay clear of pornography, stay sexually pure, read several books on marriage, get help from a professional counselor, and work through our differences instead of running from them. Laurie and I wanted to bring our full selves to each other in marriage. Values put banks on the river so that your life doesn't flood, causing irreparable damage. Determine your values.

What Are My Loads?

Common loads that most people face include school, work, parenting, friendship, and recreation. These loads change depending on the season of life. Other loads could include volunteering, debt, and possessions. And they are a lot like loads on a circuit. Not too long ago I blew the circuit in my garage because I'd overloaded it with too many amps. It can handle the freezer and sprinkler system, but when I plugged in the power washer, the circuit blew and everything shut down; nothing worked. So I called my friend Steve Rekadal, who's used to fixing my messes. Steve told me that whenever someone in the Rekadal family does something stupid, they say, "I pulled a Bob." I've become a household cliché for them, which is nice.

Everyone has certain loads they have to manage. Let's say you have five main loads, and each load requires 20 amps for a total of 100 amps. Let's also say that 100 amps are the maximum you can have on your life for it to work well. The types of loads you have in your life will vary depending on your values and stage of life, but let's say that you're married, but you're also in school, have a small family, have a part-time job, and are renting an apartment. That's a full load. Add one more thing to that load and the whole thing blows. The mistake a lot of people make is that they try to add a mortgage, second job, third child, or season tickets to an already full load. Or they fail to reduce their friendship load, which is using more amps than are available.

I see this all the time. Two adults decide to get married, they both get jobs, they have two or three kids, and then they buy a dog. But instead of adjusting or reducing their loads so they can manage their marriage, jobs, kids, and dog, they hang on to all their old friends, join a softball league, and buy a cabin. And they add about 80 amps to a circuit that's already maxed out at 100. Guess what happens when you try to run 180 amps through a 100 amp circuit: something blows and you pull a Bob.

This couple might be able to manage their overloaded life for a while, but soon they become exhausted and irritable. They may begin fighting and wonder why they don't feel close anymore. Eventually, boundaries get crossed with an attractive or sympathetic co-worker, or the children start to act out, or the car breaks down, or somebody gets sick. The overloaded circuit is in meltdown mode, and they risk losing all the things they wanted in life: a great marriage, a healthy family, a purposeful career, and physical and financial wellness. All because they lost their focus due to an overloaded life. If they overload the circuit long enough, they risk major losses, including divorce, bankruptcy, foreclosure, and rehab. Sadly, this is what happened to Lance Armstrong. The Tour de France load was so demanding that it siphoned all the amps away from his marriage, and it ended a few years later. Lance beat testicular cancer, fathered a son, and won the Tour. Then he lost his family. The downside to being as focused as Lance was to win the Tour is that it *can* blind you to other matters that need your attention. Focus is a necessary quality for success, but if it's one dimensional, you can win at racing and lose at life. Manage your loads.

What Do I Need to Stop Doing?

In his book *Good to Great*, Jim Collins writes, "Do you have a 'stop doing' list? Most of us lead busy, but undisciplined, lives. We have ever-expanding 'to do' lists, trying to build momentum by doing, doing, doing—and doing more. And it rarely works. Those who built good-to-great companies (and lives), however, make as much use of 'stop doing' lists as 'to do' lists. They display a remarkable discipline to unplug all sorts of extraneous junk."[7]

What do you need to stop doing to get your sanity and life back? I stopped accepting outside speaking and teaching roles. I commit to only two outside speaking requests per year, and I say no to the rest without guilt. I stopped doing all-day golf outings because a full day conversing with guys on a course drains me and doesn't line up with my values. I still golf on my day off, but I do it with my good friend Trent, who plays as fast as I do. We meet for coffee at my house at 6:30 a.m., and we're back home by 10:30 to enjoy the rest of the day. I sold my boat because the to-do list associated with owning a boat is endless—you have to pay for it, insure it, maintain it, equip it, fix it, gas it, use it, winterize it, store it, and stand in line at the DMV to renew it. And you get no aerobic payoff while using it. The day I sold my boat I felt amazingly free. I watched the guy tow it down the road and whispered to myself, "That guy just towed away all my headaches." (They say that a man's two happiest days are the day he buys a boat and the day he sells it.) People who buy an increasing amount of cabins, memberships, recreational toys, and properties increase their to-do list a hundredfold. Good for them, not good for me.

To reduce your to-do list, you have to develop a strong no muscle and say no without apology. But to say no to requests, invitations, and friends who overload your life, you have to know your values, and you have to stop worrying about disappointing people. You can't let people talk you into doing something you don't want to do. Most of us should say no far more than we say yes. Memorize your response so that when you're caught off guard with a request, you automatically know what to say with a smile: "Thank you so much for asking. I'd love to do it, but I won't be able to; my days are just too full." Get it down so it just rolls off your tongue, and you'll start to feel the sweet breeze of freedom. This is difficult because it often means cutting out what is good to make room for the best.

I like to prune trees, and it's a little like saying no. Laurie hates it when I prune our trees and bushes because she thinks I get carried away. We had some lilac bushes that were getting out of hand, so I bought a pruning book and read about how to prune the bushes. I read that sometimes what's needed is an "aggressive" form of pruning to maintain the health of the bush. I like the word *aggressive*, so I took out my shears and, in my wife's words, "hacked the bushes." I pruned them a full third, cut out the old growth, and when I was done, Laurie was very quiet. I wondered about it myself. But four days later we began seeing new growth sprout up, and today the bushes look better than ever.

Every year our lives grow new "activity" branches without our intending it. We grow new meetings, commitments, classes, parties, dinners, concerts, friendships, and sporting events that overcrowd and choke our lives. We hang on to these things even though they have no value. What's needed is a good pruning. We need to cut off the dead weight so that the light can come through and cause new growth.

Things I've recently said no to:

- A full day of *free* golf with hundreds of people for a local charity. (I golfed with Trent instead and was home by 10:30 a.m. to spend the rest of the day with my wife.)
- Fishing and hunting trips with guys I don't know well. (Time away for me is too precious to risk being trapped for days with wild cards.)
- Speaking at the one-hundredth-anniversary celebration of my first church. (Someone else spoke at it.)
- Officiating at my cousin's wedding. (He found another pastor to do it.)
- Counseling. (Counselees need two things I don't have enough of: time and expertise.)
- Going out socially. (It drains me. I would rather watch the Twins with my wife at home.)

- Our landline phone. (No more solicitations or monthly bills.)
- A personal blog. (Why invite more access into my already overloaded life?)
- The internet at home. (I get it at work—no more computer upgrades or monthly bills.)

What in your life can you start saying no to? The places where people typically overload their lives include the following.

People. Many of us try to maintain too many friendships and say yes to too many invitations and outings. That causes overload. Every yes to one person is a no to someone or something else. So whom do you need to say no to so that you can say yes to the people who really matter to you?

Activities. These can include your own activities, your spouse's activities, or your children's activities. I recently drove past a local school at 8:30 on a Sunday morning and saw that all four baseball diamonds were occupied, as were both soccer fields. Parents and grandparents sat on the sidelines, and I thought "People's lives are so full that 8:30 on a Sunday morning is the only free time they have left. No wonder our churches are empty and society is drifting spiritually." In the state of Pennsylvania, it's still against the law to hunt on Sundays. I think they have something there.

Ownership. Every boat, cabin, membership, machine, toy, or trinket you add to your already packed life will demand more of your time to use and maintain. So what might you need to stop owning?

Work. Most of us have to work, but some of us work too much. And no matter how much work we do, we will never be done. Many of us could work twelve-hour days every day and still not be done. At some point you have to set a limit and stick to it. Sometimes I have to ask myself, "Why did you take that project on, and who's holding a gun to your head?" Usually when I've taken on too much work it's because:

- I'm afraid someone will be upset with me if I say no.
- I'm insecure and don't want to look like a slacker to my colleagues.
- I want to control the outcomes, so I don't delegate like I should.
- I lack sufficient faith in God's provision for my future.

Everybody has limits, and nobody will say no for you. If you're overloaded and never have enough time to attend to your main values, then you've said yes to too many people, events, outings, possessions, and activities. And you're probably doing many things poorly and nothing very well. That's a formula for low achievement. So what branches do you need to prune away so you can become strong and productive again?

In his book *From Success to Significance*, Lloyd Reeb suggests that a good way to cut away the good things to make room for the *best* things is to make a list of all your roles and responsibilities and then rank them from the highest to the lowest in terms of their importance to you and your life goals.[8] The objective is to eliminate the lowest-ranking ones that do not add as much value to your faith, marriage, family, fitness, and career. Once you list all your roles and responsibilities, select the bottom three activities and unapologetically eliminate them from your life. Make up your mind ahead of time that the bottom three must go, because it will be hard to eliminate them. You have to force yourself to do it because in the long run it will be worth it.

For seventeen years, I met with three men for once-a-month prayer at a local restaurant; we became good friends. We had breakfast, talked about our families and jobs, and supported one another through hard times. A couple of the guys even kept a journal of all the prayers God had answered over the years. But for the last year and a half, our monthly meeting seemed like it took place every other week for me. And it gave me a late start to my workday, adding more pressure to an already long day. I do my best thinking and writing in the mornings, and even though we met only one morning a month, that morning cut into my best hours and made that week extra hard. I've also noticed that when I'm facing an early morning breakfast meeting when it's dark and cold in Minnesota, I don't sleep as well the night before and experience an energy letdown about midmorning.

But how do you say no to prayer time that you've shared with three good friends for seventeen years? I wrestled with it for several months, but I knew it was the right thing to do. I knew it because my leadership team had become my new small group, and we had monthly prayer times together at work. Realistically, my monthly meeting with my three friends had fallen into the bottom category, and I had to eliminate it to make room for higher priorities. It was painfully hard to let it go and even harder to face my three friends. We're still good friends, and we still call each other occasionally. But when you don't see each other or pray for each other as often, you grow apart a little. But that's life. Things change, priorities shift, workloads increase, groups dissolve, and you lose touch. But in exchange you're able to deepen other relationships that were being neglected and refocus your life based on ever-changing demands and priorities.

What Are My Strengths?

When you know your strengths, you can stop wasting time on things you're not good at. The day I realized I didn't need math, physics, or geometry to achieve my goals, I was free. God didn't wire me for numbers and graphs; he made me to be a writer, teacher, and leader. Knowing that earlier in life would've saved me a lot of shame in school. I didn't know why other students whizzed by me in math; I thought it was because I was stupid and was destined to spend my days in remedial hell. A big part of achieving is knowing what you're bad at so you know what to avoid. I'm equally bad at organizing programs, managing people, forming an agenda, and running a meeting. I muddled through that kind of stuff when I was a youth leader and pastor of a small church, but I never did any of it well. My ability to teach covered a multitude of sins. People thought, "He stinks at everything else, but he can teach, so I guess we'll put up with him." The sooner you can identify your strengths, the sooner you can strengthen them and start achieving at high levels. It's a waste of time to try to get better at things you're not good at and will never produce great results.

Thirteen years ago Scott Anderson joined our staff as a part-time custodian. He was a manager at a local McDonald's, but he was always hanging around church picking up after people. So we asked him to make it official. Eventually, he left McDonald's to maintain our buildings full time. Then we promoted him to manage our maintenance staff. Then he became the director of operations. Today Scott is my executive pastor, leads the management team, and oversees our entire staff of two hundred. What's amazing is that not only is Scott great at what he does, but he also loves it. He's great where I'm lousy, and he loves what I hate. The flip side is also true. I'm great where he's lousy, and I love what he hates.

You know what a lot of organizations do? They put people in positions where they're weak, ask them to do what they hate, and wonder why they get mediocre results. At first I didn't want to release the management of my staff to someone else, but it was one of the smartest things I ever did, because then I was able to focus all my time and energy on leading and teaching, and our church began to soar. If you would've told me thirteen years ago that Scott Anderson would be managing my staff, I would've laughed at you. That's because I was ignorant and insecure. Today I am a little less so. Without Scott, and dozens of others who have relieved me of some of my loads, I wouldn't be sitting here writing these words while gazing at a Lake Superior ship heading for port in

Duluth, Minnesota. I wish I had learned earlier in life how much I need people. Nobody achieves at high levels without the help of others. You have to narrow your focus, and that means perfecting your strengths and letting other people do the things you do poorly.

Everyone is good at something, so think about your life and ask yourself two questions: "What do I do well, and what do I love to do?" Another way to ask it is, "What comes naturally to me, and what gives me the most satisfaction while I'm doing it?" Ephesians 2:10 says, "For we are God's workmanship, created in Christ Jesus to do good works, which God prepared in advance for us to do." God has given you the ability to accomplish certain tasks well. But he's also given you the *desire* to do them. Psalm 37:4 says "Delight yourself in the LORD and he will give you the desires of your heart." God combines ability with desire, and they're unique to each individual. Max Lucado says, "You find your sweet spot at the intersection of success and satisfaction."[9]

Penny Hegseth joined our staff in 1997 as the director of our women's ministry. But after three years in that role, Penny admitted, "I found that women were not my passion. It was kind of a joke among my friends that I was planning events that I'd never go to myself. I was doing napkins and centerpieces, and I hated it." So she said, "I can't do this anymore." Her supervisor asked, "What would you like to do?"

Penny had never been asked that before, and it launched her into a whole new role that would help volunteers find their abilities and passions. She did that for four years. But then a three-part tsunami hit: her mother died, her oldest son got deployed to Iraq, and a surgeon accidently cut her esophagus during a routine procedure. In Penny's words, "I didn't recover well, and I lost my leadership edge." Even though Penny was highly valued at church and her family needed her income, Penny knew her time was up. To everyone's surprise, she officially resigned from leadership at Eagle Brook.

It's often through hardship that God gives you the space to reflect and figure out who you are and what he wants you to do. This was true for Penny. Eventually, Penny went back to school, and today she's a leadership coach who helps people find and maximize their strengths. It's like she's been reborn.

When I asked her about it, she said, "I can't tell you how energized and happy I am to have found my purpose. When I coach, I feel God's 'super' on my 'natural'! It's important that people find out who they are before they decide what they want to do. Finding your strengths and gifts is important, but when you discover your passion, that's when you're at your best." When she's coaching people, she works hard at drawing out of them what's naturally strong within them. She listens for repeated words or phrases, and she watches when their face lights up. She says, "When people find what they're naturally passionate about, they soar."

In his book *Go Put Your Strengths to Work*, Marcus Buckingham asks, "What do you love, and what do you loathe?"[10] He advises people to pursue what they love and avoid what they loathe; this is what separates those who soar from those who just survive. It drives Penny nuts when a pro athlete or a politician stands in front of students and says, "You can be anything you want to be." "No you can't," Penny says. "You can't be anything you want to be, but you can be better than you are."

So what comes naturally to you? What roles or tasks do you consistently find yourself doing well? And what lights you up and causes you to say, "I was made for this"? It could be fixing things, raising your kids, writing notes to people, baking, or designing things. A lifetime is too long to waste on something you hate.

What Season Am I In?

People and families go through different seasons. In Ecclesiastes 3:1, the Bible says, "There is a time for everything, and a season for every activity under heaven." There's the going to school season, dating season, high school sports season, going to college and being dirt poor season, graduating and facing the real world season, starting a career and getting married season. When your first child is born, you enter the season of no sleep, no money, and no sex for about eighteen years. Each season requires that you make adjustments to your loads.

For example, the season of small children is like adding a heavy-duty power washer to the circuit—raising small children requires a lot more amps than many jobs or going to school. So for that season, you have to reduce other loads in order to handle the increased load of raising small kids. When our kids were young, I didn't touch a golf club for seven years. There was no golf, virtually no social life, and very little hunting or fishing. We didn't own a home until we were thirty-four years old, because all our amps were consumed by going to school, working part-time jobs, and caring for our kids. Now my twenty-two-year-old son takes *me* golfing, the house is paid for, I have the remote control back, and it's a brand-new, wonderful season. At first it's hard, but then it pays off.

One of the biggest mistakes people make is that they fail to adjust their life and commitments based on the season they're in. They also fail to realize that each season is temporary. Being a student is one season. It's not forever. Being a single adult or a newlywed is another season, and there's a lot of freedom in those seasons to travel, explore, and play golf. But the next season of having kids and establishing your career is the most demanding season in life, and it's going to be that way for about eighteen years. No matter who you are or what your circumstance is, there is an unavoidable level of hard work associated with raising young children, and it's critical for the long-term future of your family, home, and career that you don't overload the circuit in that season and do irrevocable damage to something. People who make no adjustments in their outside commitments, spending, travel, or social life often end up breaking something very precious to them.

So what season are you in, and what might you need to say no to, get rid of, drop, or sell to reduce your load and get your life back? You can't do it all if you want to reach your goals and live according to your values. One working mom said it this way: "I am spread so thin right now that I don't think there's anything left in me to devote to anything else. I am an overworked professional, an overtired mother, a part-time wife, and a fair-weather friend." If you try to have it all, you could end up having nothing.

■You Always Have Options

Recently, I was driving to work on a Monday morning at 6:45. I was coming over a one-lane bridge with traffic inching along both ways. I glanced over and saw a young couple. He was in a suit and tie; she was in a sharp business suit. She was looking down, busy doing something; he looked tense with both hands clutching the steering wheel. In the back seat were two car seats with swinging toys to entertain the tiny passengers. No doubt they had to make a quick stop at a day care. It had probably already been a stressful day for them. Got up at 5:30, got dressed, fed the kids, let the dog out, grabbed some breakfast. Then after struggling through a ten-hour day of meetings, projects, and managing people, there's the call from work: "Honey, I need to stay late." He can hear the irritability in her response. "But what about the kids? I thought we were going to get groceries. What about supper and the laundry?" Then she's fifteen minutes late to day care, the kids look dazed, she can tell they've been crying, and all she can do when she gets home is collapse.

I looked at that little family unit on the bridge that morning and thought, "How will they ever make it?" You can keep up that pace for a while, but eventually something snaps.

You can't endure that kind of pace without doing damage to your soul and to the vital relationships in your life. The season of raising small kids is the most demanding, most precarious season in life, and people who want to survive it have to narrow their focus. They have to make hard choices and delay certain dreams because they realize that raising young kids is an enormous load that demands every extra amp they have. People in this situation often feel trapped and think there's nothing they can do about it, but there are always options. They could:

- take a leave from work
- accept a lower income level for a few years
- accept that they're going to be poor for a while
- rent instead of owning
- ask their employer for flextime
- delay their career dreams
- ask for help from parents, family, or friends
- limit or drop their social relationships and memberships
- let go of their softball leagues, trips with the girls, and other commitments from their former lives as single adults
- seek the advice of professionals or wise mentors who can help them make sound decisions
- get connected to a support group, young couples group, or neighborhood group
- get creative and ask each other what they can drop, alter, change, or reduce

Awhile back I received a letter from a young mom who wrote:

Dear Bob,
    Each time you speak about the importance of raising young children, it brings me to tears. We parents don't get many

pats on the back. However, the rewards we get are unbeliev-
able. Many people tell me how "lucky" I am to be home.
My response is usually "luck has nothing to do with it."
God placed the desire on our hearts to have one of us home
with our kids long before we ever had them. We made an
advanced decision—together. Fortunately, I get to be home,
and that is my passion. My husband teaches seventh grade
and gets up in the middle of the night three times a week
to deliver newspapers. I wait tables three nights a week and
run the newspaper business one day a week. Our two boys
are always being cared for by myself, my husband, or their
amazing grandmother.

My point is that it is not "luck." It is a choice that many
two-parent families can make. If their financial situation is
not ideal and one cannot be home 24/7, there are options.
They may need to work odd hours and jobs they may be
overly educated for. I have my master's degree and a HUGE
student loan payment. However, "I am my kids' mom!" as
Dr. Laura would say. There are always options.

I'm not saying that it's impossible for both parents of
young children to work, only that when both parents work,
something else has to give, be dropped, or get delayed. Options abound, and every season has different loads. The good
news is that every season has an end. Being a student ends,
raising young kids ends, the teen years end, mortgage payments end. There's plenty of time to work sixty hours a week,
chase all your dreams, and knock yourself out when the kids
are raised. Don't wreck your home and life by ignoring the
season you're in.

How can you tell if you're overloaded and in danger of
breaking something? Seven common signs indicate when a
person is overloaded and heading for a crash: (1) a chronic
sense that there's never enough time; (2) constant irritability; (3) physical tension in one's body, drumming the fingers,
clenching the jaw; (4) an inability to listen to and be fully
present for people; (5) the loss of laughter; (6) a sense that

you've lost control of your life; and (7) fatigue. I can always tell when I'm depleted, because I get irritable and lose my ability to laugh. Everyone has their moments, but if all you have are moments, that's a sign of a mismanaged life. It's also a sign that God might be trying to tell you something. God did not intend for you to go through life stressed out, angry, and depleted. There's a better way, but you need the faith and courage to choose it.

What might you need to drop before it drops you?

5

Give Yourself Time

Be Prepared

Have you ever sat alone at night in a study carrel, or wasted time in a mindless job, or been stuck in a marriage that's lost its zing and wondered if it's worth it? Wondered if God has forgotten you? There were so many times when I wondered if all the part-time jobs, school, preparation, and work would be worth it. Wondered if I'd ever have enough money to buy a reliable car, go on vacation, or even own a home one day. At one time the notion of leading a church of three hundred was a pipe dream, teaching grad students in the same class-rooms where my professors taught me was laughable, leading a church of several thousand was a total fantasy.

I started having thoughts of never being able to accomplish anything significant thirty years ago when I married my high school sweetheart. We were both twenty-two and had just graduated from college. After a less-than-stellar honeymoon, we packed up our 1969 Mercury Cougar with everything we owned and drove nine hundred miles from Pittsburgh to St. Paul, moved into a one-room apartment with a mattress on the floor, and fought almost every day. Neither of us had a job, I was starting seminary to learn how to become a pastor, and six months into our marriage we both thought we'd married the wrong person. It was the worst year of our young lives and was filled with a lot of anger, tears, and confusion. Somehow we survived that year and eventually learned how to accept and forgive each other. It took several years of working through conflict and pain to learn that loving my spouse meant I had to stop trying to change her and start cherishing her. That was thirty years ago.

Twenty-nine years ago on a Sunday night I was standing in front of forty people in the basement of Elim Baptist Church in Minneapolis, and I was preaching my very first practice sermon. I was dressed in a suit and tie, and I started sweating so profusely that water dripped off my nose and chin down onto my notes. It was like someone had turned on a faucet, and the people in the congregation were so embarrassed that they had a hard time looking up. When I got my feedback forms, people had written things like, "It seemed like you were a little nervous, and wet." "I had a hard time listening to you because I thought you were going to pass out." I thought I might never speak in public again, but I learned from that experience and got a little less nervous each time after that. That was twenty-nine years ago. Three years later I graduated from seminary with a master's degree, left my job as a youth pastor, and took the next step.

Twenty-six years ago I became the pastor of the First Baptist Church in Falun, Wisconsin, where most of the sixty members were elderly or infirmed and where if I *did* pass out it wouldn't have mattered much. My annual salary was eleven thousand dollars a year, we had a beat-up old car that my father-in-law had given us, and we lived in a church-owned house with burnt orange shag carpet and a woodstove for heat. Before our two kids were born, the elders took pity on us and voted to buy us a used car for one thousand dollars. One of the elders bought it from a friend of his, but it blew up three months later in the middle of January. We were on a three-day getaway traveling north of Duluth, Minnesota, when the engine blew in subzero weather. We coasted into somebody's driveway on the north shore and asked a complete stranger if he'd be willing to take us twenty miles back to Duluth to find a hotel. Laurie was seven months pregnant, so he took pity on us and drove us back into town, where we sat on the edge of a dingy hotel bed with no car and very little money.

With our first child on the way, we decided we needed to get a reliable car, so we called a taxi, sold our broken-down car to the taxi driver for one hundred dollars, took a Greyhound bus 130 miles to St. Paul, and asked my dad to pick us up at midnight at the bus depot. We spent our entire life savings of eight thousand dollars on a new stick shift Subaru, which we drove back home the next day. But during those five years in Falun, Wisconsin, I learned how to write messages, lead a church, fix cars, run a bulletin-folding machine, and get along with deacons. After those five years, I wasn't sure I wanted to be a pastor for the rest of my life, so I went back to school.

Twenty-two years ago I became a student again at Penn State University, where I was accepted provisionally into the speech department, which meant they didn't think I'd make it. Twenty-six of us enrolled in the doctoral program that fall, and I was the only one *not* to get a teaching assistantship. An assistantship would have paid eight hundred dollars a month and would have waived my out-of-state tuition. We had two small kids and were renting an apartment, and the only job I could find was raking leaves for our apartment complex for four dollars an hour. I was a thirty-one-year-old man with a master's degree, and I was raking leaves for four dollars an hour. My boss, Lance the landscaper, wouldn't even entrust me with the push mower. I could've mowed circles around Lance. Occasionally, Laurie would stroll the kids over to visit Daddy, who was raking leaves for a living. I had to choke down my ego and just believe that someday it would all pay off. Laurie earned a few dollars a week watching three small children, and eventually she found a part-time job managing some student apartment buildings—collecting rent, fielding calls, and managing the books.

One February night our apartment building caught on fire. We woke the kids, ran out into the cold, and huddled in the stairwell of an adjacent apartment building. The only two items I grabbed as we hurried out the door were my wallet and a computer disk with my dissertation on it. Some Taiwanese students took us in that night, and we found a motel the next morning. We had a lot of water damage, but we were able to salvage most of our pitiful belongings. That was just one of the dozens of times I wanted to quit school and find a small church somewhere that I could lead for the rest of my life.

Some people have asked me how I made it. It was simply the belief that God had led me there and that eventually all the hard work would pay off. I didn't know how or when, but I believed that if I hung in there and did the hard work first, the payoffs would come later.

Eventually, I was awarded an assistantship at Penn State. That happened on the same day I was sitting on top of a mountain ridge overlooking Happy Valley, and a beautiful ten-point buck ran past my deer stand. It stopped briefly to look back at something, and my trusty ol' 30-06 rifle didn't let me down. I can still hear the shot echo across the valley on that gorgeous November morning. When those two magical events happened on the same day, I took them as a sign that God was still with me and that all the hard work was starting to pay off.

Later that year I was hired by the speech department to teach seminars at schools and hospitals throughout the state of Pennsylvania. I also taught undergrads introductory speech classes, but I hated every minute of it. I've learned that you have to try different things in life to find out what you don't want to do; it helps crystallize who you are and what God's wired you to do. It was time for me to leave academics and get back into the church world. The exact day my committee signed off on my dissertation, I left town. I had them mail my diploma. The nickname for Penn State is Happy Valley, but those three years were the unhappiest years of my life. I had pockets of joy followed by depression, fear, and ongoing poverty. That was twenty-two years ago.

Nineteen years ago I became the pastor of the First Baptist Church of White Bear Lake. I was thirty-four years old. We had two staff members, two worship services, a congregation of 350 people, and I was scared to death. I hoped that we would grow to 400 during the next five to ten years, but in my gut I had serious doubts. I had no experience leading a large suburban church, and I was plagued by self-doubt and chronic anxiety. I was also in such severe conflict with my associate pastor that I didn't know if I'd make it past the first year. The daily power struggles and hurtful arguments made me feel like I was trying to run a race with two severed hamstrings. Many nights I woke up at 2:00 a.m. lying in a fetal position with a tight chest and intense fear. All I could manage to do was put one foot in front of the other and just try to survive. One year later he left, and the elders wondered if I had what it took to lead their church. But they gave me a chance, and nineteen years later it seems like something out of a storybook.

During the first decade or so of my adult life, I was in and out of school, always broke, working part-time jobs, trying to limp along with old cars, stuck in tiny offices and no-name towns. I had no hope or promise that any of the schooling, work, sacrifice, and eating of peanut butter and jelly sandwiches would ever pay off. There were so many points along the way when I was tempted to quit. For example, I can remember sitting in the basement of Patee Library at Penn State as a thirty-three-year-old student looking at reels of microfilm of eighteenth-century preaching and wondering, "What am I doing here? The whole world is passing me by, and I'm sitting down here day after day wasting my life in utter obscurity." I sat in that basement eight hours a day, Monday through Friday, for a full year with no promise that my dissertation committee would reward me with a degree after giving three years of my life to it. The basement windows of Patee Library had steel bars across them, and I felt like I was sitting in a prison. It seemed as if the only person who really knew or cared about me was my wife. For those three years I was a number, a nobody, of no importance to anyone. The only thing I hung on to was an inner belief that someday, somehow it would all pay off. That, and some wise words my mother-in-law, Mary Lou, gave me.

At a particular low point, she said to me, "Bob, the days are long, but the years are short." Isn't that true? Her mother had said that to her when Mary Lou was living in a tiny apartment with three little girls all in cloth diapers. Mary Lou had to keep reminding herself that the days are really long, but the years are really short. And they are. The days of being a college freshman seem endless, but then you graduate—and you realize that the years are short. The days of raising young kids are endless, but then they're gone; the years are short.

The days at Penn State were long, but what I didn't realize was that those three short years shaped my entire understanding of secular society and how to speak to it with God's truth. I thought I was getting a degree in speech, but God put me there to get a degree in life. I didn't realize that during that time God was building something *in* me so that he could do something *through* me. Since then I've had opportunities to travel the world, teach students how to preach, lead one of the best churches in the nation, assemble a great staff, and watch our kids move responsibly into adulthood. And I get to go home every day to my very best friend of thirty years.

It took a long time, but Happy Valley has finally come to the Merritt home. Through it all I've learned a couple of key lessons.

■Time Plus Preparation Equals Opportunity

I find it interesting that Jesus spent thirty years preparing for three years of public ministry. That's 90 percent of his life preparing, 10 percent performing. What was he doing during those thirty years? Luke 2:52 says, "Jesus grew in wisdom and stature." The most perfect model of humanity spent thirty years preparing for three years of worldwide impact. God put Moses in a desert for forty years to prepare him to lead six hundred thousand Jews out of slavery, because time plus preparation equals opportunity. Some of us can't wait forty days.

Sometimes people wish that God would bless them with opportunities before they're ready to handle them: managers who want to oversee more people, builders who want larger crews and bigger projects, teachers who want to be the principal, assistants who want to be head coaches, pastors who want bigger churches. Sometimes God spares us embarrassing failures by withholding certain opportunities until we're ready.

> I find it interesting that Jesus spent thirty years preparing for three years of public ministry. That's 90 percent of his life preparing, 10 percent performing.

I mentioned that out of twenty-six incoming students at Penn State, I was the only one who didn't get an assistantship that first semester. I prayed for one, needed one, sucked up to all the right people for one, but nothing happened. In hindsight, had I received an assistantship and been required to teach speech courses to undergrads while pursuing my degree, I probably would have dropped out of the program, because I wasn't ready. In all my years in school, I had never taken one speech course, and yet I was hoping to teach it to undergrads. I watched several of my colleagues buckle under the pressure of trying to do their own course work while teaching classes at the same time. I had the luxury of having an upperclassman mentor me, invite me into her classroom, and share her lesson plans with me. By semester's end, I was ready. And second semester I was given an assistantship that had been forfeited by one of my classmates who didn't make it.

I honestly believe God was protecting me from failure by giving me time to prepare. It takes time and preparation to grow in wisdom and stature. Sometimes it feels like you're in a desert and things aren't going your way, but God does some of his best work in deserts. Sometimes God has to build something in you before he can do something through you, and that takes time and preparation.

Walmart founder, Sam Walton, once said, "People have the impression that Walmart was something I dreamed up out of the blue, but not so; like most overnight successes, it was about twenty years in the making."[1] The UCLA Bruins basketball dynasty of the early '70s won ten NCAA Championships in twelve years under John Wooden. But how many years had Wooden coached the Bruins before winning his first championship? Fifteen. Wooden needed two things: time and preparation. So he worked in relative obscurity, studying, recruiting, and sharpening his skills before becoming history's most legendary college coach. Proverbs 21:5 says, "Good planning and hard work lead to prosperity, but hasty shortcuts lead to poverty" (NLT). There's no such thing as an overnight success.

Take the lottery, for example. Did you know that nearly one-third of lottery winners go bankrupt? Why? Because they didn't do what Jesus did. They didn't take the time or have the experience to grow in wisdom and stature; they never developed the skills or character necessary to handle money. Victoria Zell won $11 million in 2001 and is now serving time in a Minnesota prison, her money gone. Zell was convicted in 2005 of an alcohol-related collision that killed one person and paralyzed another. Evelyn Adams won the New Jersey lottery in 1989 for a total of $5.4 million but gambled it all away. She's broke and lives in a trailer. Bud Post won $16 million in 1988 but now lives on food stamps. He says, "I wish it never happened; it was a total nightmare." A former girlfriend sued him, and his brother was arrested for hiring a hit man to kill him. Post even spent time in jail for firing a gun over the head of a bill collector.

Financial planner Susan Bradley writes, "For many people sudden money causes disaster. There's a widely held belief in our culture that if people had more money their problems would be over; often it causes more problems than it solves." Most lottery winners become losers again because they never built the skills necessary to hang on to their winnings.[2] The Bible says that good planning and hard work, not hasty shortcuts, lead to prosperity. Time plus preparation equals opportunity.

■ "If" Always Leads to "Then"

Early on in the Bible, God was trying to set up the Israelites for success. God said, "*If* you faithfully obey the commands I am giving you . . . *then* I will send rain on your land . . . so that you may gather in your grain, new wine and oil . . . and you will eat and be satisfied" (Deut. 11:13–15). He continued, "*If* you carefully observe all these commands I am giving you to follow—to love the LORD your God, to walk in all his ways and to hold fast to him—*then* the LORD will drive out all these nations before you, and you will dispossess nations larger and stronger than you" (vv. 22–23). And finally, "So be careful to do what the LORD your God has commanded you; do not turn aside to the right or to the left. Walk in all the way that the LORD your God has commanded you, *so that* you may live and prosper and prolong your days in the land that you will possess" (Deut. 5:32–33).

These verses have an if-then relationship: *if* we obey, *then* good things will happen; *if* we do things right, *then* God will bless our lives; *if* we don't swerve to the right or left, *then* we will prosper and prolong our lives. God has set up the world in such a way that everything is connected. If I do A, then B will follow. Andy Stanley calls this the principle of the path: "Direction, not intention, determines destination."[3] It means that whatever path I'm on—not good intentions, not luck, not even prayer—will lead me to a certain destination. If I'm on the path of overspending, that path will lead me to debt and bondage. No matter how much I pray about it, blame others for it, or wish it weren't true, if I get on the path of overspending, it will lead me to financial ruin. Every choice I make today is connected to an absolute outcome tomorrow. The outcomes might not be immediate, but they are certain. Stanley says, "Today's decisions create tomorrow's experiences."[4] Whatever decision I make today will absolutely impact my life tomorrow, for good or bad, for gain or loss.

When our kids were in kindergarten, they each brought home a six-inch-long seedling spruce tree in a plastic bag. I planted them on the side of our property and then forgot about them. Today, nineteen years later, those two trees are twenty feet tall and offer shade to our yard, privacy from our neighbors, and nesting for the birds. Today's decisions create tomorrow's experiences. A always leads to B; *if* always leads to *then* because everything is connected. What might you need to plant today that nineteen years from now will be something strong and beautiful? What might you need to dig up and get rid of today that nineteen years from now will save you from pain and regret?

> Today's decisions create tomorrow's experiences.

Everybody wants the good and the gain, but not everybody is willing to plant the seeds and stay on the path that leads to those things. I've noticed that the paths I got on twenty years ago are still affecting my life today: staying in school, writing a 250-page dissertation, fixing old cars instead of buying new ones, saving money, choosing to stay sexually pure, remaining faithful in marriage, and raising our kids. Many people don't see immediate payoffs to those kinds of things, so they get bored and impatient. They think they're missing out on life, so they swerve off the path and do something really foolish like quit school, buy on credit, move in with a girlfriend or boyfriend, take on enormous debt, form an addiction, or have an affair. They don't realize that those choices will take them down a predictable path that will keep them from the very things they want: financial stability, a fulfilling career, an intimate marriage, and family love.

In Deuteronomy 5:32–33, the Bible warns, "Don't swerve to the right or to the left; do what's right and good in the Lord's sight, so that it may go well with you" (author paraphrase). God's desire is that *it may go well with you*. It's not God's fault if we swerve off the road and end up in a ditch. God's promises are absolutely true, that *if* we stay obedient and unswerving, *if* we consistently do the right things, *if* we stay on the right path today, *then* he will prosper and prolong our lives tomorrow. It's not a guarantee that accidents and illnesses won't occur along the way, because we still live in a broken world, and nobody is immune to setbacks. But as a general principle, God promises to bless and benefit those who stay on the right path, because *if* always leads to *then*.

Henry Cloud talks about a woman who hated her job and had always wanted to practice law. But when he asked her why she wasn't pursuing it, she said, "Law school takes three years." She didn't understand that she had chosen a path that would continue to lead her away from her dreams.

Cloud said, "And you hate what you're doing now?"

"Yes, but it'd take me too long to get a law degree."

She needed to get on a different path so that her future destination would be a favorable one. Cloud asked her, "Do you plan to be alive three years from now?"

The woman said, "I certainly hope so."

"So three years from now will come no matter what, right?"

"Right."

Cloud said, "Here's my question: When that day comes three years from now, do you want to have a law degree or do you still want to be hating your life?"[5]

If I study, then I learn. If I learn, then I increase knowledge. If I increase knowledge, then I have opportunities. If I have opportunities, then I gain skills. If I gain skills, then I have options. If I have options, then I'm happy. If I'm happy, then I'm healthy. If I'm healthy, then I achieve. If I achieve, then

I have influence. If I have influence, then I have impact. If I have impact, then I have purpose.

But if I quit, then I fail. If I fail, then I'm dependent. If I'm dependent, then I'm not free. If I'm not free, then I'm unhappy. If I'm unhappy, then I'm unhealthy. If I'm unhealthy, then I'm miserable. If I'm miserable, then I'm poor and lonely, because nobody wants to hire, marry, or hang around dependent and miserable people. *If* always leads to *then*.

Every decision is connected to an outcome, and the decisions we make today absolutely determine our experiences tomorrow. So what are you doing today that will make your tomorrow better? Because A always leads to B; *if* always leads to *then*.

■Everything Has an Ending

I never thought grad school would end, but it did. I never thought renting would end, but it did. I never thought working part-time jobs would end, but they did. I never thought the kids would grow up and leave home, but they did. I never thought mortgage payments would end, but they did. I never thought twenty years would pass, but they did, just like that.

Twenty years from now is going to come. In twenty years, will you be educated, free of debt, married to the same person, and proud of your kids? Will you have your house paid off, a rewarding career, and lifelong friends? Or will you be in a financial and relational ditch somewhere? Twenty years seems like a long time, but twenty years from now is going to come, and it comes faster than you think—like next week.

I promise that what you do today determines who you become tomorrow. So what seed do you need to plant, what class do you need to register for, what bad habit do you need to drop, what diet do you need to begin, what exercise program do you need to start, what apology do you need to make, what sin do you need to confront and overcome? What do you need to do *today* so that five, ten, or twenty years from now you'll be healthier, happier, and freer?

6

Find Your Rhythm

Increase Your Consistency

Ten years ago my wife and I traveled to a dairy farm in Amery, Wisconsin, to look at a litter of Chesapeake Bay retrievers. These are not cuddly house pets; Chessies are large, hearty dogs bred to withstand the icy waters of northern climates. When you read about Chesapeakes, you read things like, "Can swim for hours in frigid water; are die-hard retrievers; have a mind of their own; trainable, but a little slow to learn; will make you prove that you're the boss; are more aggressive and willful than other retrievers; are not recommended as house dogs; have an oily coat that sheds; tend to drool." My wife claims I love our Chessie because she's a lot like me: trainable, but a little slow to learn.

When Laurie said that the dog would be a house dog, the farmer said, "But these dogs drool and shed. And they stink." Laurie looked at me and said, "I'm used to that. Plus what's the point of having a dog if you can't have it in the house?" So we brought the dog home, and the rule was that she would be kenneled at night, and when she wasn't outside roaming the backyard, she'd be confined to the wood floors in the kitchen area.

For a year we held firm. But eventually we softened and extended Bear's territory from the kitchen to the living room, but by no means would she ever be let upstairs. I insisted that we had to have an area kept clean from hair, drool, and vomit. "Never will this dog be let upstairs," I said.

A year later the kennel was gone and she was sleeping upstairs right outside our bedroom door. And our daughter had given her free reign of her bedroom, sometimes letting her jump right up on the bed. I thought, "How did this happen?" Then I started getting the sad, droopy eyes from my wife and daughter. But I insisted, "No way. There is no way this dog will ever be allowed in my bedroom."

"But she loves you," they'd say. "Look how she follows and adores you. She's already upstairs. What's the harm?"

I said, "She's an animal and smells like it."

For a full year I held firm, until one night our bedroom door was left ajar. Bear nosed her way in, and she quietly lay down as close as she could to my side of the bed. I reached down to grab her scruff in protest, but instead I gently stroked her head. She let out a sigh of relief, and I lay there thinking, "I've lost all control." That became her spot, and I've never admitted this to my family, but eventually it became a comfort to me to have her there.

These days she sleeps downstairs on our good sofa, violating yet another rule I vowed would never be broken. And it's like clockwork: about 7:00 p.m., she gets up from wherever she's lying on the floor, walks over to the sliding door that opens to our deck, and stands there until one of us opens it. Then she waddles her aging body down the stairs, trots back to the woods where she's been trained to go, comes back, and gives a single bark at the door. When we let her in, she walks over to where we're sitting on the couch and stares at us, willing us to get off the couch so she can climb on and

settle in for the night. What do we do? We forfeit the couch
and go sit somewhere else. It's embarrassing.

But over the past ten years, Bear has worked her way so
deeply into my soul that I can hardly stand the thought of
her leaving us one day. Every morning for the past ten years,
she's been the first one to greet me in the morning—with a
full-body dance. It doesn't matter if the day before she got
yelled at or swatted on the rump. My furry friend greets me
with a full-body dance *every* morning—circling the kitchen
table a few times, bumping into furniture, whacking my legs
with her gigantic tail that with one sweep can clear an entire
coffee table of magazines. If I'm wearing blue jeans and a
sweatshirt, she knows it's my day off, and the dance turns
into whimpers and whines that don't stop until I take her
out back to play fetch; that's after she licks the bottom of
my coffee mug of course. (Bear and I have coffee together,
because my wife drinks tea.)

On Sundays when I come downstairs dressed in nice slacks
and a button-down shirt, the dance is less dramatic, because
Bear knows it's all business. I feed her a quick breakfast and
I'm out the door. When I get home six hours later, I change
my clothes, eat some food, and head for the couch to take a
nap. Bear knows the routine, and she knows that now isn't
the time for fun. She quietly walks over, lies down next to
me on the floor, lets out a big sigh, and stays still until she
hears me stir about forty-five minutes later. She raises her
head, stands up, and sticks her big, wet nose in my face. If
I don't get up right away, she plants her big paw on my arm
and coaxes me off the couch with a series of playful, irresist-
ible growls and yelps. She wants me to take her out back to
play fetch. It's as if she's got the Sunday afternoon rhythm
programmed into her brain.

There are many things I love about dogs. They're loyal,
teachable, communicative, and happy—pretty much everything a cat isn't. But I think a dog's greatest asset is that
they embody these qualities every minute of every day. They

can't help themselves; it's who they are. You never have to worry about a dog being moody or holding a grudge. Dogs don't go through phases or have meltdowns. And when it comes to forgiveness, nobody does it better—they forgive immediately and completely every time. They provide a consistent level of stability in a world that is consistently unstable and unpredictable. More than once I have lain down beside Bear after a hard day, buried my face in her soft fur, and gotten strength from her strength. When I sit to write, she lies quietly at my feet until I get up from my seat. Then she heaves herself up, follows me to the fridge, looks inside with me, and then follows me back to lie under the table until I get up again. If I go visit the bathroom, she pulls herself up, follows me ten paces down the hallway, lies down outside the door, and then follows me back to the living room. Her mood is always the same, her habits are the same, her daily dance is the same, and how she works a pheasant is the same. When Bear's tracking a pheasant, I know exactly what to expect by watching her body language and tail. I understand her rhythm, and she understands mine.

Those who study behavioral science would say that a dog's emotional intelligence (EQ) is off the charts because they are transparent, likeable, loyal, dependable, and emotionally stable, and they're like this all the time. There's no deviation; they are predictably this way. Travis Bradberry and Jean Greaves are cofounders of TalentSmart, the world's leading provider of emotional intelligence tests and training. They have found that EQ is the number one predictor of professional and personal success. They've learned that while a person's IQ is important, "people with the highest levels of intelligence (IQ) outperform those with average IQs just 20 percent of the time, while people with average IQs outperform those with high IQs 70 percent of the time."[1] That gives me hope. It means that intelligence can take you only so far. People who are highly intelligent but who can't manage their emotions, have unpredictable mood swings, and lack loyalty don't fair well in life. Again, a dog's greatest asset is that they're the same every minute of every day, and there's no deviation; you know exactly what you're getting and when you're getting it. Dogs embody predictable rhythms and routines that make them one of the most dependable creatures on the planet.

Becoming more consistent in life increases a person's overall effectiveness. And the way you become more consistent is by establishing a healthy rhythm that fits who you are and enables you to meet life's challenges. The good news is that everybody has a rhythm; the bad news is that not everyone's rhythm is healthy or productive. Some people need to change their rhythm to increase their productivity, lower their stress, and enrich their relationships. If successful, they just might be able to move from the kennel to the kitchen to the master bedroom.

Rhythm Is Not Random

Some people chafe at the notion of establishing predictable rhythms and routines because they say they're confining and squelch creativity. Such people value random, not rhythm. So they make random plans, have random jobs, keep random hours, eat random food, pursue random relationships, and get into random marriages. Random is king because it's spontaneous and free. The problem is that random is often unreliable and undependable. You can't hire random because you never know what will show up or when it will show up. You can't put random on a team because they're off doing their own thing. Random is hard to pin down because random rarely stays put. Random bounces around and goes with the flow, which is nice if you're sixteen, living at home, and driving your parents' car.

A close cousin to random is organic.

Recently, I asked one of our musicians what he was trying to accomplish on the platform because I thought that whatever he was doing was missing the mark. He said, "Well, it's kind of organic."

I said, "What does organic mean?"

He said, "I can't really tell you; as soon as you define it, it's no longer legit." Then he said something about creating a certain "vibe" that leader types don't get. "It's kind of vibey," he said.

Don't get me wrong. I'm okay with random, organic, and vibey as long as you show up on time and deliver the goods. Too often, though, random leads to an ill-prepared, mismanaged, never-enough money, always-running-on-fumes kind of life.

> Rhythm . . . is predictable, dependable, punctual, and hireable. . . . Rhythm gets things done.

Rhythm, on the other hand, is predictable, dependable, punctual, and hireable. Rhythm keeps office hours. You can locate rhythm. You can count on rhythm. Rhythm gets things done.

Rhythm achieves; random falls short. Rhythm reaches its goals; random doesn't even know what a goal is.

For his book *Good to Great,* Jim Collins studied the qualities that separated good companies from great companies. He says, "In the great companies we were struck by the continual use of words like, *consistent, focused, disciplined, rigorous, dogged, determined, diligent, precise, fastidious, systematic, methodical, workmanlike, demanding, accountable,* and *responsible.* These words peppered articles, interviews, and source materials on the good-to-great companies, and were strikingly absent from mediocre ones."[2]

Incidentally, *random, organic,* and *vibey* didn't make the list.

Some people say that adherence to predictable rhythms, routines, and structures stifles creativity. Untrue. You can be creative within structure, and a consistent structure actually enhances creativity.

■Establishing Your Own Rhythm

The most perfect model of humanity to ever walk the planet, Jesus, adhered to a predictable rhythm. Matthew 14:23 records, "After he had dismissed them [the crowd], he went up into the hills by himself to pray." In Mark 1:35, the author writes, "Very early in the morning, while it was still dark, Jesus got up, left the house and went off to a solitary place, where he prayed."

Part of Jesus's predictable rhythm was that after he spent time and energy being with people, he went away by himself to rest and pray. He would just disappear, and it actually became an annoyance to his disciples. "Simon and his companions went to look for him, and when they found him, they exclaimed: 'Everyone is looking for you!'" (Mark 1:36–37). Translation: "Why do you keep sneaking away like this? We have places to go, people to heal, important things to accomplish."

There will always be those who don't understand your rhythm and will try to get you to change it to fit their agenda. And if you don't change, they may even question your commitment or work ethic. But they are not you, and they don't have to manage your life; only you can manage your life. If you allow someone else to dictate your rhythm, your pace will become unsustainable, and you won't be able to accomplish your goals.

Allowing someone else to dictate your rhythm is actually an indication that you haven't thought through your priorities. If you set your priorities, then you will follow a predictable rhythm that enables you to accomplish them. You have limitations of time and energy, so you have to make sure that your daily rhythms and routines serve your goals and priorities. Jesus didn't heal, save, or teach everybody. Luke 5:15–16 says, "Crowds of people came to hear him and to be healed of their sicknesses. But Jesus often withdrew to lonely places and prayed." In other words, Jesus routinely left things undone and needs unmet. He often withdrew to lonely places while the crowds were still pining to see him. Even Jesus was subject to the limits of time and energy, which is why he established a rhythm.

Paul said, "Whatever you have learned or received or heard from me . . . *put it into practice.* And the God of peace will be with you" (Phil. 4:9). What are the predictable practices that could bring more peace and well-being to your work environment? What are the predictable rhythms that could bring more peace to your relationships? What are the predictable practices or rhythms that could bring a more consistent and healthy balance to your studies, diet, exercise, and sleep? People who eat right, exercise, and stay out of debt don't have more willpower than others; they just have better rhythms that they have practiced for so long that they've become normalized behavior—part of their daily routines.

So once you've identified your top goals (I have five top goals), you have to figure out the most effective way to accomplish them. And that will require establishing a predictable rhythm in six main areas.

Your Soul

One of my goals is to have a vital relationship with God. But that doesn't just happen; I have to find a place where I routinely meet God. And I have to meet God in this same place often enough so that it becomes a normal rhythm in my daily life. When it becomes part of my rhythm, I no longer have to fight it or think about it because it is a normal part of my daily life.

But I need a specific place. For me it's at my desk at work, where first thing every morning I read a chapter out of a soul-inspiring book and a chapter or two out of God's Word, and then I spend a few minutes in quiet reflection and prayer. It's during those moments that I get nuggets of wisdom and comfort from great authors and from God's Word that set the tone for my whole day. This morning I read in Proverbs 19:8, "He who gets wisdom loves his own soul; he who cherishes understanding prospers." Those who wish to prosper in their work, studies, relationships, and finances will seek the best wisdom in the world. My books, Bible, and God are waiting for me in the same place every morning. We have a daily appointment.

One of the tools that has helped me and thousands of people in our church is a Bible-reading plan that keeps you on a schedule and helps you establish a rhythm. But we have found that reading plans that try to get you through the Bible in one year are too rigid and defeating. If you miss a day, you scramble to catch up; miss two or three days and you give up entirely because you're so far behind.

The goal in reading your Bible is not to get through it in a year. It's to sit with God for a few minutes several times a week and soak in his wisdom. If you miss a day or two or three, God still loves you the same. *It's not a race; it's a relationship.* Sometimes I'll sit with one paragraph or even just one verse because God is using it to speak to me. (People who are just getting started can access several modified Bible-reading plans on our website: eaglebrookchurch.com.) I've noticed that when I'm on vacation or it's my day off, I seldom spend time like this with God. The reason is because I don't have a set time and place; vacation takes me out of my rhythm. To nourish your soul, you have to get into a predictable rhythm.

Your Body

You need a rhythm to stay physically fit. I belong to a health club partly because having a specific place to go keeps me in a rhythm. The physical act of taking a right turn onto the freeway after work and walking into the health club seals the deal for me—as much as I hate it. If I go home, I never exercise. Home triggers a different flow for me. Home is not where I work or work out; home is where I relax, eat meals, and watch TV with my wife and dog. I take the right turn onto the freeway four or five times a week after work. But it's different for everyone. Many people exercise in the morning and do it at home.

Jim Citrin at Yahoo! surveyed twenty CEOs and asked them about their daily rhythms. Eighty percent of them wake up at 5:30 a.m. or earlier. More than 70 percent of these CEOs exercise in the morning, while 15 percent find a way to do it during the day. Only two of the executives admitted to not exercising on a regular basis.[3]

The place or environment where you exercise is very important. Hitting the treadmill at 5:30 a.m. in a cold, dark basement without music, TV, or a fireplace is like a prison sentence and not conducive to establishing a long-term rhythm. One of my colleagues works out in her basement at home, but she created a room that's warm, welcoming, and vibrant. She painted the walls a bright color and has a thirty-two-inch plasma TV and a CD player, because that's the only way she can endure the monotony of a thirty-minute workout. But that's her place, six days a week.

In the summer, I alternate between health club workouts and biking. I ride the same twenty-mile loop every time because I'm familiar with every bend, rut, hole, and blind curve in the road. The one time I deviated from my route I almost got killed. I came to a stop sign at an overpass, and I thought it was a four-way stop. As I peddled onto the bridge to go left, a speeding car came over the rise. I braced myself for impact and looked away because there was no way the car could miss me. But it did miss me. I don't know how or why, but I believe God intervened in that moment. I almost lost my life that day simply because I broke my rhythm and wasn't familiar with the route.

Your body needs exercise to function at optimal levels, but willpower isn't enough. You have to establish a rhythm that becomes as routine as eating and sleeping.

Your Work

When it comes to work, I'm an office guy. It's not that I can't work at home or in a coffee shop, but the physical act of going to my office triggers the work mode in me. When I'm at work, I work; I don't waste time, mess around, or fritter away half the morning surfing the web or chatting in the hallways. I do those things over lunch or at the end of the day. I am most efficient in that environment partly because all my support systems are there: my assistant, colleagues, books, papers, and internet. Once I leave the office, I'm done. I leave the place where I work, which allows me to detach from it, relax at home, and attack my work afresh the next day. If I regularly take work home, my energy wanes, my passion leaks, and my creativity drops. I end up getting the blahs, which is a signal that my rhythm is out of whack. A good rhythm allows your mind, body, and soul a chance to replenish themselves for maximum efficiency.

Bestselling novelist Stephen King writes about his work rhythm: "There are certain things I do if I sit down to write. I have a glass of water or a cup of tea. There's a certain time I sit down, from 8:00 to 8:30, somewhere within that half hour every morning. I have my vitamin pill and my music, sit in the same seat, and the papers are all arranged in the same places. The cumulative purpose of doing these things the same way every day seems to be a way of saying to the mind, you're going to be dreaming soon."[4]

When John Grisham first began writing, he had a certain routine: "I had these little rituals that were silly and brutal, but very important. The alarm would go off at 5, and I'd jump in the shower. My office was 5 minutes away. And I had to be at my desk, at my office, with the first cup of coffee, a legal pad and write the first word at 5:30, five days a week."[5] His goal was to write one page every day. Sometimes that would take ten minutes, sometimes an hour or two. Then he'd begin his full-time job as a lawyer, which he no longer does. At one page a day he'd have a 365-page novel by the end of the year.

In his autobiography *Surprised by Joy*, C. S. Lewis writes:

I would choose always to breakfast at exactly eight and to be at my desk by nine, there to read or write till one. If a cup of good tea or coffee could be brought me about eleven, so much the better. At one precisely, lunch should be on the table; and by two at the latest I would be on the road (walking). The return from the walk, and the arrival of tea, should be exactly coincident, and not later than a quarter past four. Tea should be taken in solitude. At five a man should be at work again, and at it till seven. Then, at the evening meal and after, comes the time for talk, or failing that, for lighter reading; and unless you are making a night of it with your cronies there is no reason why you should ever be in bed later than eleven.[6]

One of my friends does his best writing in a coffee shop away from his office, phone, and staff. He does most of it in one day. He's virtually a mole during that entire day—out of sight and mind. I write in stages over several days because in between stages (even at night) creative ideas pop into my subconscious thinking. Some of my best creativity happens when, after I've written awhile, I take a walk, ride a bike, or swim. My mind is seeded with thoughts, but then my subconscious is freed up, the oxygen begins to flow, and ideas come flying out of nowhere. This is known as oscillation. You get up from your desk, walk around, climb a flight of stairs, come back, work for a while, get up, and oscillate again. It increases the oxygen and blood flow and refreshes your mind. Some of my best material floats into mind while I'm on my bike or on a walk. What are your work rhythms, and are they working?

Your Team

Now, none of this means you can establish your work rhythm in a vacuum. Very few of us have the liberty of establishing our rhythms exactly the way we want to. When you are a part of a business, school, or corporation and you're receiving a paycheck every two weeks, you can't live by your own rhythm and expect everyone else to work around it. Nobody has the freedom to establish their own rhythm to the neglect of others who work with and around them. Everyone has to attend impromptu meetings, help with unexpected projects, stay late sometimes, or miss a workout. That's life.

I once had an upper-level staff person waltz into work at 10:00 a.m., read the paper in his office until 10:30, do some work, meet someone for a lengthy lunch, stroll back in, check his emails, attend a meeting or two, and leave at 3:00. He said that he liked to work from home, which is fine if his work showed it, but it was lacking on many fronts. He didn't understand our need for him to have regular office hours, model it to those reporting to him, and be a part of the team. He's no longer on our team.

A good team outperforms a group of individuals every time. A team has more ideas, a diversity of skills, and far more synergy than any single person. You can't beat a good team. But building a cohesive team takes time, which is why longevity is so critical to a business, family, or friendship. We've lived in the same town and same house for nineteen years, and the stability that has brought to our children, marriage, neighborhood, friendships, and church is immeasurable. I heard some advice long ago that helped me: plant a tree in your yard and don't move; watch it grow for at least ten years. I planted more than forty trees on our property, and I've watched them grow for nineteen years. It's one of the best things I ever did.

When you plant your roots, you begin to build a network of team support. For example, I get my tires from Harvey, my car fixed by Vince, my hair done by Becky, my teeth done by George, my medical needs checked by Dale, my money managed by Greg, and my Sichuan chicken prepared by Chuck. I don't have to waste time flipping through the Yellow Pages or wondering if I'm going to get ripped off. They know me, and I know them. We're a part of each other's life and rhythm. My wife has told me that if I die before she does, she would never remarry because it would take her too long to train another husband. It's that "trainable, but slow to learn" thing. The thought of it makes her weak.

I feel the same way about our staff. They know my rhythms so well, and I know their rhythms so well, that the thought of starting over with different people is exhausting. None of us is perfect, and all of us have annoying quirks, but we know each other's quirks and have learned to work with them. We can read each other's nonverbal cues and know the triggers that tend to spark conflict. When one of us hurts another unintentionally, we can discern it quicker and patch it up. When you don't know someone well, little hurts can fester, pile up, and morph into resentment and anger.

When you work with a team of people long enough, they begin to establish their rhythms around your rhythms, and that creates efficiency. When people know your rhythms, they know where to find you and how to plan their day around you. If your rhythm is sporadic, nobody can plan meetings with you, count on you, or involve you in their decision making. Collaboration becomes hit and miss, stop and start, and nothing gets done.

Your Marriage

Rhythm makes for healthy marriages because you know when to move in and when to back off, when to give the person space and when to tackle hard issues. If you don't know or respect the other person's rhythm, you or your spouse can become offended, and neither of you gets what you need or want. But when you understand and respect each other's rhythms, there is flow and predictability.

Laurie and I used to get upset with each other on Sunday afternoons because we didn't understand each other's rhythm. I came home from church at 12:30 p.m. needing a warm meal, a nap, and a workout; that's all I wanted or needed. She, on the other hand, wanted to know everything about the morning, how it had gone and whom I had seen; she needed someone to talk to. Our rhythms were out of sync. But instead of talking about each other's rhythm, we just assumed the other could figure it out. "It's obvious what I need, and how can you not know that?"

Finally, we had an inspiring conversation about it, and ever since that day, Sunday afternoons have become the sweetest part of our week. We've learned that if Laurie gives me time to replenish with a warm meal, a nap, and a workout, then I've got the energy to meet her needs for conversation and time together. It took us about fifteen years to figure that out.

Your Children

Consistency and rhythm are things children need for them to feel secure in the world. One cold fall morning I stopped to pick up my brother-in-law Oz to go hunting, and his two little boys were out at the bus stop with about five other kids. Their backpacks were all lined up in a row. You know the drill. The first one at the stop plops his backpack down first in line to hold his spot, and you move someone's backpack at the risk of getting beaten up. Children know intuitively that it's a mortal sin to move someone's backpack.

So just to mess with them a little, I went over and said, "Whose backpack is first in line?"

"That's Bart's," they all responded in unison. "Bart's is always first," they said.

"How come Bart's is always first?"

Little Oz said, "Cuz Bart's dad leaves for work early, and he puts Bart's backpack out here at like 5:30 in the morning."

I asked, "Well, where's Bart right now?"

"Oh, he never comes out until the bus comes," they said.

I thought, "Well that isn't fair. Bart's in there sipping hot chocolate and watching cartoons while the rest of the kids are out here freezing." So I said, "What do you say we put Bart's bag at the very end of the line?" Their jaws dropped, and nobody said a word; all their little faces had a look of *Is that even legal?*

Finally, little Oz said, "You can't do that, Uncle Bob."

I asked him, "Why not?"

His voice quivered as he said, "Because Bart will cry."

Understand that nobody *liked* that Bart was always first in line, but what they liked even less was changing the rules. Consistency is very important at the bus stop.

And if moving a backpack at a bus stop is a big deal to kids, think of what moving from school to school, church to church, or home to home does. As much as kids rail against bedtimes, curfews, and rules, research shows that children who have consistent boundaries and limits do much better in school, stay out of trouble more, and have better relationships than children who don't. Given all the challenges, pressures, and fears children are faced with in society today, I caution parents to think carefully about uprooting their kids from the stability of their home, church, and friends.

In his book *Family First*, Dr. Phil states, "One of the major themes you'll hear me repeat throughout this book is that the phenomenal family has a certain rhythm—a beat that communicates, 'This is where we're from, this is what we stand for, and this is what we do together.' Children need this rhythm in their lives, and it's unsettling to them when they don't have it. This factor is absolutely critical to the well being of your family."[7] These rhythms can include a family game night, mealtimes, birthday celebrations, storytelling, bedtime prayers, and going to church together. Dr. Phil states that it's these predictable activities and patterns in your family life that serve as psychological and behavioral anchors for your values and beliefs and that provide your children with a sense of stability and security.[8] Establishing a predictable rhythm is a major factor in helping children gain the confidence they need to navigate a tough world.

Seasonal Rhythm

Do rhythms change depending on the season of life? Yes, but certain rhythms will never change based on a person's hardwiring. I will always be most creative in the mornings. I will never gain energy from social outings. I will always need regular periods of solitude built into my rhythm to restore. I will never allow myself to be ill-prepared when giving a message, speech, or interview. I will always need space after a weekend of leading and speaking. Exercise will always be a part of my rhythm, even on vacation.

God made you in such a way that you need a daily rhythm, weekly rhythm, monthly rhythm, and annual rhythm. At 9:30 every morning I get my only cup of coffee. I reward myself with that small pleasure every day. During lunch I sit in our cafeteria and enjoy the playful banter with staff from all departments. Then at the end of the day, after my workout, I go home to eat, relax, unwind, and read or watch TV with my wife. I love those two and half hours from 6:30 to 9:00 p.m. It's my daily Sabbath.

Every Friday is my weekly Sabbath. I don't go to work, talk to staff, answer my phone, or overload my day with projects. Obviously, some home projects need to get done, but a lot of things get left undone. It's why we'll never own a second property. Life's too short.

My monthly rhythm is somewhat dictated by seasonal events like Easter, Christmas, and fall. But I've gotten into a monthly groove where I speak three weekends in a row and then have one or two weekends off from speaking. I go hard and then let up, go hard and then let up.

For my annual rhythm, I have a monthly planner that I use to block off vacation and travel time a full year in advance.

If it doesn't get on the calendar, it doesn't happen. This also helps my staff members plan their year. After a long, hard season, I reward myself and my family with a getaway of some sort. Living in Minnesota, we've found that going south somewhere for ten days in February helps us thaw out and rejuvenate our souls. When my kids were teenagers, I made a commitment to take them each somewhere fun once a year to make sure I was connecting with their lives. I have a six-week summer break that I use for vacation, writing, and fishing in Alaska, and I always take a fall hunting trip. These are the things that keep me alive. People who are going at Mach speed and fail to build in regular intervals of rest and recovery are out of rhythm and won't sustain over the long haul. Your life should look less like a straight line and more like a roller coaster with regular peaks of output followed by valleys of rest. You don't have a work life and a home life. You have one life, and everything's intertwined.

Breaking the Rhythm

Should rhythms ever be broken? Yes, but only when it's worth it. Vacation is worth it; kids' functions are worth it; birthday parties, milestone celebrations, and pets that wreak havoc with rhythms are worth it. I've learned that I have to make time for things that I don't have time for because that's where God often shows up, that's where surprises and adventures happen. You can't be so rhythmic and calculated that you miss the rich moments that occur outside the daily routine. So there's a place for random, as long as random isn't a lifestyle.

One of the reasons people have such a hard time returning from vacation is that they've been out of their rhythm. We've said to our kids many times, "You'll feel better once you get back into a rhythm." After I've been away, it usually takes me a day or two to get back into my rhythm at work, and once I'm in it, my efficiency goes up, I find my groove, and I'm on my way. But those first couple days back are always hard.

One of the ways to ease the pain of reentry is to maintain your exercise, sleep, and diet rhythms while on vacation. Rhythms need to become a part of your lifestyle even on vacation. I haven't seen a New Year's Eve midnight for decades. Why? Because watching the ball drop isn't worth yanking me out of my sleep rhythm.

■ The Payoff of Rhythm

At this point you might be saying, "What a regimented, boring life Bob must lead; that's not for me." Well, it all depends on what you want out of life. Finding a healthy rhythm helps you say no to things that don't coincide with your goals. And it gets you in a groove that increases your efficiency. This creates space or margin in your life because you're on track and not constantly pulled in several directions. So you're able to find time to spend with your spouse or family on a daily basis. You have a legitimate day off because you're not working sixty-hour weeks. You're physically and financially fit, and you're on a purposeful path that makes you feel good about yourself and others. In short, you're not living on fumes due to a random, disorderly life. The payoff to rhythm is huge.

> Every person I've met who's accomplished something great in life applied the discipline of rhythm for one simple reason: they had to.

Every person I've ever met who's accomplished something great in life applied the discipline of rhythm for one simple reason: they had to. Every great musician, writer, student, speaker, leader, athlete, builder, teacher, and doctor is well acquainted with this discipline. Ask any successful person if the countless hours of studying, rehearsing, and practicing were easy, and they'll tell you they were brutally hard. But they'll also tell you those hours paved the way to a great life.

Many years ago the legendary golf pro Gary Player was hitting balls off the practice tee one morning, and the first ball he hit went 280 yards straight as a bullet. A guy in the gallery just within earshot said, "Man, I'd give anything to be able to hit a golf ball like you."

Gary walked over to the guy and said, "No, you wouldn't."

The guy said, "Yes, I would. I'd give anything to hit like that."

Gary said, "No, you wouldn't. You wouldn't be willing to do what it takes. You have to rise early in the morning and hit five hundred balls until your hands bleed. Then you stop, tape your hands, and hit five hundred more balls. The next morning you're out there again with hands so raw you can barely hold your club, but you do it all over again. If you do that through enough years of pain, then you can hit a ball like that."[9]

Player won more than 160 professional golf tournaments and is a member of "the big three"—along with Jack Nicklaus and Arnold Palmer—who dominated golf through the 1960s and 1970s.

Ninety-nine percent of life is dull and routine, but that 99 percent of dull and routine eventually shows up in the 1 percent that everyone sees. It's what made Gary Player, and those like him, go from good to great.

Bottom line, rhythm increases your efficiency and effectiveness, which means you're able to accomplish things at work or school that you couldn't otherwise. That leads to more opportunities, more success, and more relational and financial stability. People begin to value and trust you, and they give you greater freedoms and privileges. You can take guilt-free vacations and know that your house is in order back home. Rhythm might seem difficult at first, but it gets you where you want to go.

7

Have Barbed-Wire Discipline

Use Small Tugs

Have you ever faced something in your life that seemed so insurmountable that you thought there was no way to change it? Most of us will face an enormous problem at some point in life that seems too big to solve: college, graduate school, a dissertation, job loss, addiction, an out-of-control teenager, a failed dating life, an unfair boss, a weight problem, the list goes on and on. And when we look at the enormity of our problem, we're tempted to avoid it and watch another six hours of TV.

It's like the big ball of barbed wire that for fifteen years sat in our back woods at home. Long before we had purchased this property, someone had taken down a long section of barbed-wired fencing, rolled it up, and dumped it on our property. This enormous pile sat in our woods all gnarly and enmeshed into the ground—impossible to move. For fifteen years I looked at that tangled-up mess. It annoyed me every time I was in the backyard, but there was nothing I could do about it. Occasionally, I'd go over to the pile, study it, walk around it, and tug on it, but there was no way to move it. Sometimes I'd stand on our back deck and just stare at it from a distance.

So I thought maybe if I prayed really hard, God would remove it for me; that didn't work. Maybe my kids, whom I've spent hundreds of thousands of dollars feeding, clothing, insuring, and educating, would surprise me one day and have it all cleaned up; that didn't happen. Maybe my wife, whom I love and adore, would clean it up; not in a million years. Maybe if I just ignored it and tried to block it out of my mind, it wouldn't bother me anymore. Didn't work.

So one day I stood there looking at that ugly mess, and I finally made a decision that each time I was in the woods, I would break off a piece and put it in our garbage can. I wasn't sure if the pile had more wire than I had days left on earth, but I couldn't stand it any longer. I had to do something.

So little by little I started pulling on a corner of that enormous pile. Every time I was in the woods I'd break a little section off, carry it to the garbage can, and then forget about the pile until I was back in the woods another day. Normally I just dive into something and get it done, but this beast was so entangled and huge that to try to tackle it all in one day or one week or one month seemed overwhelming and defeating.

For several months it looked like nothing was happening; two or three months went by, and it seemed pointless. But I kept at it, bit by bit, little by little, and about five months into it, I began to notice a difference. A couple months after that, whole sections began breaking off, and I remember the day when I knew that pile was mine. It took me about fourteen months, but that pile is now completely gone. For fifteen years that pile junked up our woods and affected my mood, but now it's gone. I think the garbage man's a little upset with me, but it's gone.

I want to ask you, "What's your big ball of barbed wire? And where do you need to start tugging?"

What is it in your life that seems so overwhelming that every time you think about it you just want to crawl into a hole and forget it? Maybe when you think about it you say to yourself, "I can't overcome that, I can't get rid of that, I can't do that." And you're right; you can't do it, at least not all at once. But here's the truth: no matter what your pile is, *you can do something.* You can start pulling on a little corner of that pile, and bit by bit you can overcome whatever problem you have. It might take five, ten, or fifteen years, but overcoming starts by pulling on the pile: one payment, one class, one counseling session, one AA meeting, one phone call, one act of forgiveness, one dollar in savings, one pound lost, one page written, one tug at a time.

It's Never Too Late to Start Tugging

I have a colleague who is one of the best in the country at what she does. We've worked together for eight years, she is on our leadership team, and she is one of the most respected leaders in our church. She's on top of every aspect of her professional and personal life, except one. Her weight. She used to work out and be in good shape. But then over a span of several years a perfect storm blew into her life that threw her off her game: she and her husband were surprised by a third child when their second was just fourteen months old; she returned to a sixty-plus-hour work week fresh off maternity leave; her best friend died at age thirty-one; and her marriage was strained, to say the least. Amy was a mom to three kids, a rising star at 3M, and a worn-out wife who never got to fully grieve the loss of her best friend. Something had to give, and it was her devotion to her own fitness.

Eight years later she was tired of being out of shape and decided to do something about it. Amy is goal oriented, so she set a goal to enter a 5K race in four months and downloaded a training program that would lead her to that goal in small increments. The voice on the download became her daily companion as each morning he led her step by step. On the first morning it was a one-minute jog on the treadmill followed by a two-minute walk. Amy said, "At about thirty seconds I thought I was going to die." A 5K seemed like an impossible reach. But she kept pulling on the wire. Two mornings later she was back on the treadmill for a two-minute jog. Again, she wanted to barf and die. A week later she popped into my office with a big smile and said, "I'm up to three minutes."

Amy's also a Diet Coke–aholic—people actually give her cases for her birthday. Most mornings she cracks open the first can before 9:00 a.m. She recently admitted to me that on a typical day she would drink sixteen cans. That's 1.5 gallons each day. I can't drink 1.5 gallons of anything each day. But now I see her carrying water around, and she's down to six cans a day.

For Amy, accountability is huge, so she let me and others know of her fitness goal, which is extra motivation. I think everyone in the office knows about it, because as much as she wants this for herself, she wants to show the rest of us that she can conquer her problem.

About two months in, Amy's moment of truth came. She was going off on a weekend up north to scrapbook with a girlfriend. Keep in mind, this was February in Minnesota, and they were staying at a place with no fitness center. I tried to catch her before she left to warn her not to fall off the wagon, but I missed her. I fully expected her to return having taken two steps backward. But while her friend and the other "scrappers" slept warmly under their covers, at 6:00 a.m. Amy heaved herself out of bed in the dark and put on her jogging clothes. In her words, "I used to look at people who jogged in the dark and cold like they were crazy; now I was out there with them." When she told me about it, I couldn't have been more proud. She is up to fifteen minutes on the treadmill, has lost eight pounds, and recently finished her first 5K run. She proudly announced, "I finished in 1,473rd place out of 1,759 runners. I wasn't last!"

Now she has to make this a natural part of her daily rhythm so that it becomes a natural part of her life. According to the Human Performance Institute, 90 percent of our behavior is unconscious, which means we do things without thinking, like crack open a Diet Coke at 9:00 a.m. and keep it going until 9:00 p.m.[1] Those who work out five times a week usually don't have more willpower; they just have better habits that have become a part of their unconscious rhythm. At some point you have to face the problem and start attacking it.

■It's Never Too Big to Start Tugging

No matter who you are, you will likely face problems and barriers that will tend to paralyze and defeat you. Leaders come to our church and attend our conferences, and often the response I get from them is, "But, Bob, our problems are so huge and our resources are so limited that there's nothing we can do to fix them." And these leaders are right; there is nothing they can do to fix them, at least not all at once. But what they can do is start pulling on a corner of the pile.

All the improvements we've made to our church campuses, staff, messages, media, musicianship, and board structures started by tugging on a corner of the pile. We used to have one part-time music director who played trombone. Today we have five full-time worship leaders who lead with electric guitars and whose musicianship is concert quality. That didn't happen overnight. That took nineteen years of tugging. No matter how impossible the pile and how limited the resources, every church leader could:

- improve their messages by a little bit each year—anybody can do that without cost.

- add accomplished musicians to their stage one at a time.
- set some simple goals for each ministry area and start measuring them.
- deal with an attitude problem of a staff member, board member, or volunteer.
- replace the carpet, paint the walls, or fix the door.

The question is, what's your tangled-up mess? What drives you so nuts that every time you look at it or think about it you wish it were different? That's a good place to start. Cutting back from sixteen to six Diet Cokes is a good start. Jogging one minute instead of none is a good start. Reducing your caloric intake by one hundred calories a day is a good start. What's stopping you? You can't change everything all at once, but you *can* change something. It's not about big breakthroughs and swinging for the fences. It's about getting a little bit better every day.

■Small Tugs Repeated Over Time Produce Big and Lasting Results

This is the lesson behind barbed-wire discipline, and it's true about anything in life: small tugs repeated over time produce big and lasting results. You don't lose weight all at once; you lose it in small increments over time with exercise and smaller meal portions, and you make healthy habits a daily lifestyle, even on vacation. It's true of building a business, getting through school, growing spiritually, eliminating debt, or accumulating wealth.

The wealthiest man in the ancient world, Solomon, wrote these words to his sons: "He who gathers money *little by little* makes it grow" (Prov. 13:11). Monetary growth doesn't come from a sudden windfall, hitting it rich, or playing the lottery. It comes from small deposits, repeated over time, resulting in big gains.

Small Tugs in Marriage

This is also true in marriage. Great marriages are built by small deposits repeated over time. In his book *The Relationship Cure*, Dr. John Gottman calls these little deposits "bids."[2] A great marriage is not primarily the result of mastering active listening techniques, understanding personality differences, or even having a date night once a week with your spouse. All those things can certainly help, but Gottman says that great marriages grow out of the hundreds of little interactions that couples have every day. A bid is any verbal or nonverbal expression sent from one spouse to another. It could be a comment, gesture, look, touch, hug, kiss, smile, or greeting. It could be "How are you?" or "I like your hair." Those are positive bids. Negative bids include things like a scowl, a rolling of the eyes, or a negative comment.

Gottman says that married couples give each other hundreds of bids (or tugs) every day. Most of them are just little things that don't seem to matter much, but over time they build up to either strengthen or destroy a marriage.

For years, Laurie would give me a positive bid when I came home from work. Every day she'd say, "How was your day?" But even if it was a good day, I'd send a negative bid back like "Lousy" or "I don't want to talk about it," and I did it without thinking. Sometimes I just ignored her, and without knowing it, I was telling her, "Leave me alone, don't bother me, your question is unimportant to me." Not a big deal initially, but over time my negative bids sucked the warmth and love out of our marriage. Not only was I pushing Laurie away, but I was also giving myself permission to be an idiot. I fell into what Gottman calls a "crabby state of mind." Have you ever fallen into the habit of being a grouch? Being grouchy had become a part of my unconscious behavior. But it really was a choice. I was choosing to be crabby—a basic "knob" as my friend Trent calls it. (That's short for doorknob.)

143

No more. These days Laurie will say, "How was your day?" and I'll usually give her a hug and say, "It was a good day. How was yours?" Her positive bid is met with a positive bid back, and that sets the mood for the entire evening. Little things like reaching over to hold her hand while watching TV, lifting my head and showing interest when she talks, responding with a nod and an uh-huh instead of silence are little positive bids or tugs that have put the spark back into our marriage. Solomon once observed, "A cheerful look brings joy to the heart, and good news gives health to the bones" (Prov. 15:30). How's your look? How's your smile? A smile says, "I like you, I'm happy to be around you, I'm in a good mood." These are tiny, little bids that Solomon says bring joy and health to our relationships.

> Great marriages . . . are the result of hundreds of positive tugs that over time produce huge gains.

Gottman found that couples headed for divorce ignore their mate's positive bids 82 percent of the time, while couples in stable marriages ignore them only 19 percent of the time.[3] He says that healthy couples tend to "turn toward" each other. They physically turn toward and acknowledge each other's bids. Couples in dying marriages tend to turn away or ignore each other's bids.

So great marriages are not the result of huge breakthroughs, extensive therapy, or understanding deep personality differences. They are the result of hundreds of positive tugs that over time produce huge gains. Marriages that fail generally don't fail because of one major blunder. Failed marriages are usually the result of the hundreds of small put-downs and little neglects that build up over time. Nobody *suddenly* falls out of love; nobody *suddenly* chooses to have an affair; nobody *suddenly* decides to get divorced; nobody *suddenly* decides to dump their best friend. Those failures are the culmination of hundreds of little tugs that were ignored or rejected along the way. You build a marriage one *bid* at a time; you bury it one *dig* at a time.

Small Tugs in Business

Small tugs repeated over time also produce big gains in business. In the mid-1980s, Toyota determined to build a luxury vehicle that would do the impossible: beat BMW and Mercedes-Benz at their own game. But they wouldn't do it through huge breakthroughs or strokes of genius. Toyota was dead set against silver-bullet solutions or finding the one big magic pill. Instead, they achieved success through what Toyota calls continuous, incremental, evolutionary improvement—by small, incremental tugs. Matthew May, who studied the secret behind Toyota's success with the Lexus and wrote a book on it, writes:

> When the LS400 made its debut in 1989 it stunned the automotive world and set a new luxury standard. The facts made history: in every category rated by *Car and Driver*, the LS400 trumped the best of the best: BMW 735i and Mercedes 420SEL. The Lexus LS400 was five decibels quieter, 120 pounds lighter, 17 miles per hour faster, got more than four more miles to the gallon, and retailed for $30,000 less than the BMW 735i.[4]

How did they do it? Japanese engineers dismantled the top-end BMWs and Mercedes, laid out every part, and used only the best ideas for the LS400. Ichiro Suzuki oversaw the project and demanded that the new car had to be faster, quieter, lighter, easier to handle, more comfortable, and more fuel efficient. The engineers and technicians said it wasn't possible. Greater speed needs more power, which means a heavier engine, which demands more fuel, and makes more noise. But Suzuki insisted on working the details to find a way.

Late in the process, the car was still too heavy, consumed too much fuel, and wasn't quiet enough. The solution: build an engine cast almost entirely from aluminum. Now it was light enough and fuel efficient, but it was still too noisy. Every moving part was examined in detail, and they found that it was the shaft that was making all the noise. The shaft has two parts in all rear-wheel cars. Toyota's solution: build a perfectly straight one. The noise disappeared, and the impossible happened: the LS400 became the bestselling luxury car worldwide. May writes, "Take a lesson from the Lexus story. If you want big leaps, take small steps. If you want quantum impact, sweat the details."[5]

■The Pile That Made Nehemiah Cry

There once lived a man, Nehemiah, who faced an enormous "barbed-wire pile." But he understood the principle that small tugs repeated over time produce big and lasting results.

The nation of Israel was built by Kings Saul, David, and Solomon around 1000 BC but was destroyed by the Babylonians four hundred years later. It says in 2 Chronicles, "The Babylonians burned the house of God and broke down the protective walls of Jerusalem, and burned all its buildings and destroyed all its valuable articles" (2 Chron. 36:19, author paraphrase). In other words, the city was completely flattened, and the Jews who survived were scattered throughout the region and sought refuge wherever they could. This brings us to Nehemiah, who found refuge eight hundred miles away in Persia and who became employed by the Persian king.

Several years later Nehemiah's brother came to visit him with some men. Nehemiah questioned them about the surviving Jews and the condition of Jerusalem. "They said to me, 'Those who survived the exile are . . . in great trouble and disgrace. The wall of Jerusalem is broken down'" (Neh. 1:3). The Bible says that when Nehemiah heard this news, he sat down and wept for days. But then he got up and started tugging. Nehemiah shows us that there are four critical steps to overcoming seemingly insurmountable problems.

Step 1: Fast and Pray

Sometimes when a problem is so overwhelming, all you can do is sit down and cry. And that's what Nehemiah did. He cried and mourned, the Bible says, "for days." But after he wept, he "fasted and prayed before the God of heaven" (Neh. 1:4)—again, for several days. When Nehemiah received the devastating news that his homeland was destroyed and his people were suffering, his impulse was to fast and pray. Whenever you become so overwhelmed that all you can do is cry, that should be a signal to fast and pray. And this is step 1 in the process of overcoming any problem.

I don't like to fast, but I've begun to fast and pray more often, especially when our family or church is facing obstacles—piles that are so impossible that if God doesn't show up we will completely fail. My wife and I fasted for the protection of our kids when they were going through high school. We fast when they face a major crossroad. But I don't like to fast.

My dislike for fasting is directly connected to my love for food and my rituals surrounding food. I have breakfast rituals. Almost every day before work, I sit down with a bowl of Raisin Bran or granola topped with a sliced banana. With my newspaper in one hand and the remote in the other, I flick between *SportsCenter* and *The Today Show*. At work I have my daily brew of morning coffee with the precise mix of cream and sugar. And that's just breakfast. I have lunch, dinner, and post-dinner rituals as well. What I eat is as important to me as when, where, and with whom I eat.

Which is why fasting is a major bummer for me. Food is so central to my life that when I deliberately set it aside for the purpose of prayer, it's a true sacrifice. But God honors it every time. During a fast, you are saying to God that your pile is so enormous that without his help you won't be able to overcome it. So instead of taking in food that day, you're going to take in more of God. Whenever food pops into your mind, or you have a hunger pain, or you forgo a food ritual, you are reminded to pray for your pile, and I'm telling you, it works. God honors it, God responds to it, and he intervenes in ways that wouldn't happen otherwise.

Nehemiah shows us that the first part in the process of moving piles is to fast and pray. By the way, Nehemiah was a man just like us. We tend to think that these biblical characters were superhuman or superspiritual—they weren't. They were normal people like you and me.

For example, the Bible says that "Elijah was a man just like us. He prayed earnestly that it would not rain, and it did not rain on the land for three and a half years. Again he prayed, and the heavens gave rain" (James 5:17–18). When Elijah prayed for the rain to return, the Bible says that he prayed *seven* times. After the seventh time, a cloud formed in the distant sky, and it began to rain after three years of drought. But the key phrase is *Elijah was a man just like us*. He wasn't superhuman or superspiritual. He didn't have a special "in" with God. *He was just like us.* The biblical characters cried and mourned. They experienced pain, loss, and doubt just like us. The difference is Elijah prayed seven times. Nehemiah fasted and prayed for days. I often pray about something once and then give up.

Does that mean God doesn't respond to single, Hail Mary prayers? No. But God does place a higher value on relationship than he does single-shot requests. Like most earthly fathers, our heavenly Father responds more to those who are in a daily, loving, trusting relationship with him than those who just want something from him. Elijah conversed with God repeatedly; Nehemiah sat and conversed with God for several days. And the God who did wonders through them is the same God who will do wonders through us.

But then Nehemiah ended his season of prayer, and he went to the king to ask for a leave of absence so he could travel to Jerusalem to see the destruction for himself. He traveled eight hundred miles to Jerusalem and spent three days examining the city to assess its condition. And this is the second step in the process of moving piles.

Step 2: Assess the Condition

Nehemiah questioned his brother about the condition of Jerusalem, and then he went to the city himself to find out everything he could. And while his men waited outside, the Bible says that Nehemiah examined the walls and gates himself. He walked around the city and studied it. He wanted to see it firsthand because he wanted to know exactly what he was dealing with. After he had fully inspected and assessed the ruins, he came back to his men and said, "You see the trouble we are in: Jerusalem lies in ruins, and its gates have been burned with fire" (Neh. 2:17). A key part to overcoming any pile is to assess its condition and be honest about it. Nehemiah's assessment was that the city, people, and heritage were in big trouble.

But people fail to assess the problem all the time. A teenager is in full rebellion, but instead of assessing the problem and facing the harsh realities of what's causing the rebellion, the parents look away and figure it's just a phase. Or a marriage is in disarray, and the pile of resentment, anger, and abusive talk keeps growing higher and higher. But instead of looking into it and trying to assess what's broken, the husband and wife assume everything will eventually work out. Or a couple sees their pile of credit card debt get higher and higher. But instead of sitting down with a financial planner to assess their financial condition, they keep spending beyond their means and think it won't hurt them. Or someone burns through relationships. But instead of making an honest assessment of their relating patterns, they assume everybody else is the problem.

After you've sought God in prayer, the next part in the process of moving the pile is to be honest about it. As hard as it is to face the facts, you need to stop pretending, stop avoiding, stop ignoring, and say, "You know what, I'm in trouble. My marriage is in trouble, my health's in trouble, my kids are in trouble, my finances are in trouble, my walls are in ruin, and the gates have been burned." A key part to overcoming anything in life is to access the condition and be honest about the facts.

When the economy collapsed during 2008 and 2009, I refused to look at our 401k, partly because there really wasn't anything we could do about it. But after avoiding it for six months, we knew we had to assess the condition of our financial world so we could figure out what to do next.

It was painful. Forty-three percent of our life savings was gone, vanished into thin air. It was a hard reality, especially when you've tried to do everything right. Our lifelong pattern was to save 10 percent or more of every paycheck, give 10 percent or more, and live on the remaining 80 percent. Greg, our financial guy, came over to our house with the grim news. But he was reluctant to show us the real numbers. Finally, I said, "Greg, I want to see the numbers. I want to see what we had, what we lost, and what the final figure is. Give it to me straight."

We were never rich to begin with, but when Greg showed me the numbers, I was quiet. But I had to see it, feel it, and face the reality of it, because there was something about seeing it printed on paper that made it real. Then Greg said, "I've done some calculations. If you retire at age sixty-five [I'm fifty-three], and you keep saving at your present rate, you'll run out of money by seventy-two."

I said, "That's not good is it?"

He said, "No, it's not, unless you're planning on dying before seventy-two."

Almost right away we started thinking about a new strategy, because life is full of adjustments, isn't it? You have a plan, but then something unexpected happens, so you have to adjust and create a new plan. Laurie and I had made plans to remodel our kitchen and entryway—we even had the architectural design for it. Immediately, we put that on hold. Then we decided on what I call "an aggressive form of saving." We knew we had to nearly double the amount we saved each month for the next ten years. I also made a mental adjustment to the possibility of working longer than I had originally planned.

You can't possibly know what actions to take without assessing the condition of your pile. When I'm seventy-two, I might become a greeter at Walmart, but I'd like it to be my choice. Assess the condition of your pile.

Step 3: Take Ownership

Even though the Babylonians had destroyed the Israelites' city and life, when Nehemiah learns about the condition of Jerusalem, this is what he prays: "LORD, . . . I confess the sins we Israelites, including myself and my father's house, have committed against you. We have acted very wickedly toward you. We have not obeyed the commands, decrees and laws you gave your servant Moses" (Neh. 1:6–7). Nehemiah knew that whenever the Israelites drifted from God and became disobedient, God often withdrew his protective blessing and allowed neighboring nations to exploit them.

So Nehemiah takes ownership of the problem. Sure the Babylonians are dirtballs, sure they destroyed the city and ruined their lives, but Nehemiah doesn't even mention them. He says, "I confess the sins *we* Israelites, including *myself* and *my* father's house, have committed against you. *We* have acted very wickedly toward you. *We* have not obeyed." Nehemiah knows that blaming somebody else for their problem will never solve it, so he says to himself, "Maybe we had a part in our own demise. We have to own it to get over it."

People who succeed in life rarely blame their teachers, bosses, co-workers, roommates, or spouses. Instead, they take ownership. People who take ownership for their financial problems roll up their sleeves and go back to school, put in long hours, work two jobs, learn new skills, become faithful employees, and refuse to buy on credit. People who are physically fit get off the couch, join a health club, walk during their lunch hour, and refuse to blame their upbringing, slow metabolism, work schedule, or cold winters for poor fitness. People who have solid marriages work every day at holding their tongue, managing conflict, getting help, and asking forgiveness. They refuse to blame their spouse for their problems and understand that the only person they can really change is themselves. They ask, "What's one thing *I* can do today that will improve my marriage?"

It's easy to think that people who are financially sound, physically fit, and relationally happy just fell into it or were just plain lucky, but that's not true. They took ownership for their lives. If your knee-jerk habit is to blame someone or something—spouse, friends, pastor, church, economy, parents, boss, roommate, traffic cop, landlord, upbringing, Republican or Democratic Party—for your current pile of disappointments, you will never get anywhere. You will never make improvements to your life, because ultimately only you can improve your life. Everybody gets wronged once in a while, but if you're *always* getting wronged, and it's *never* your fault, then I hope you like your pile. At some point you have to take ownership.

Step 4: Add a Little Bit of Faith to a Little Bit of Action

In chapter 4, Nehemiah's enemies are really putting on the heat, and the builders are getting shot at. So Nehemiah makes a statement that's really a summary of how he lived his life: "Remember the LORD . . . *and* fight for your brothers" (Neh. 4:14). I love that. "Trust in God, but fight like mad. Trust in God, but don't be a pansy. Trust in God, but pick up your sword."

Nehemiah lived by the adage that when you add a little bit of faith to a little bit of action, miracles happen and things get done. It was the one-two punch of *trusting* as if it all depends on God and *working* as if it all depends on us that helped them overcome. It's not all God, and it's not all us. We need to work with God to attack the pile. And in chapter 6 it says, "So the wall was completed . . . in fifty-two days. When all our enemies heard about this and all the surrounding nations saw it, our enemies lost their self-confidence, because they realized that this work had been done with the help of our God" (vv. 15–16). When you add a little bit of faith to a little bit of action, you can overcome impossible odds.

On September 6, 2005, the most impossible, most awful news invaded Jennifer Silvera's life. Her husband, Officer Shawn Silvera, father to one-year-old Madelynn and two-year-old Jordan, kissed his family good-bye, said "I love you," and left his home in St. Paul for his afternoon shift. A few hours later, three uniformed police officers stood on Jennifer's porch, visibly upset. Traveling in excess of 110 mph on a freeway not far from their home, a twenty-six-year-old felon used a stolen car as a weapon, purposefully aimed the car at Shawn, who had stop sticks out, and hit him. Shawn's body was thrown farther than a football field, his neck breaking instantly from hitting the windshield. A year later at the trial, the accident reconstructionist would testify that Shawn had only six-tenths of a second to get out of the way.

> Nehemiah lived by the adage that when you add a little bit of faith to a little bit of action, miracles happen and things get done.

In her amazing book, *Believe*, Jennifer wrote about the many days and nights she spent just trying to exist: "Life has taken on a new color: Gray. At present, I don't see in color. Nothing is bright or exuberant. Nothing stands out. I feel disconnected. As the months pass, I continue to feel removed from life. Time does not heal. Life as I have known it has ended, and now I'm waiting for it to actually be over. The pain is always here; it doesn't go away."[6]

One day Jordan approached Jennifer and said, "What's that there, Mommy?" pointing to a tear on Jen's face. "What's this one?" he asked again, pointing to another tear while wiping it away. "There's a tear on your eye, Mommy. Are you sad, Mommy?" Jordan gently prodded. Jennifer writes, "I could barely nod. Quietly he touched my face with his chubby toddler finger and placed my teardrop on his own eye." "There's a tear on my eye now, Mommy," he said. "I'm sad too."[7]

Jennifer writes about sitting beside Shawn's dead and bleeding body in the ambulance at the accident site—his blood-soaked pant leg, black-and-blue marks on his face, the traffic backed up for miles on the freeway. "*This is not my Shawn.* But that's when the final detail came to me—his scent, strong and sweet. Then I knew it was him. This was my Shawn. His arm was still warm. It looked unharmed, mildly tanned by the late summer sun. I couldn't help but touch it. I wanted to kiss him. I was afraid to. *Can I kiss death?* Would it be appropriate? I kissed my fingers instead and touched his mouth."[8]

Jen writes about her silent screams, her hatred for life, and her inability to find joy in things that would normally be joyful: "Each morning I put my feet out of bed wondering, *Is this really my life? Will I ever feel good again?* Quickly followed by, *I don't want to do this anymore—there isn't one day that I don't feel lonely and sad.*"[9]

Midway through her book, Jennifer begins to talk about healing and hope. She found that while her pain will never go away and her life will forever be altered by Shawn's death, healing does come, and when something impossible invades your life, it's important to start moving.

She writes, "When Jordan was a little over three years old he tiptoed to my bed one morning and with his nose near my cheek asked, 'Mom, should we wait until the sun comes up to say good morning?' It was 6:02 a.m. Tugging at my arm he said, 'Wake up, Mom. Let's get into the morning.'

"As I crawled out of bed his words stuck in my mind. *Get into the morning.* What did that mean to me? It meant to put effort into my day, face it, live it, learn from it, move with it; I needed to *start moving.* I stood in front of my bathroom mirror and told myself, 'Move, Jennifer. Just move. All you need to concentrate on is moving.'"[10]

Jennifer found that the activity of journaling was therapy for her, but moving can be as simple as making a cup of coffee or taking a walk. "Nearly anything is better than nothing. Healing is work. God's Spirit works healing in us when we work to heal." She met a friend who'd also been widowed. When Jen asked her how she coped, she said, "Baking. You write, I bake. I baked so many cookies after Tom died I had to start throwing them away."[11]

Jen said:

> Moving doesn't . . . make everything okay, but when I move I sense God moving in me, and with me. [So] that's what I did. Morning after morning. Hour after hour. Minute after minute. . . . Even though my life connection with Shawn had died, I was still very much alive—so I kept moving. I found that when I moved, God moved. I found strength in God's promise from 2 Corinthians 12:9: "My grace is sufficient for you for my power is made perfect in your weakness." God's grace is sufficient for me. . . . By simply moving and letting Christ take over, even though I felt weak I was becoming strong. This was Christ's strength in me.[12]

Jen found that when she started moving—when she added a little bit of faith to a little bit of action—her impossible pile of grief started to shrink. Not overnight, but bit by bit Jennifer began to live again, and trust again, and love again. Four weeks ago she met me down front after a service and introduced me to her family—and to a gentle, young man named Steve. She gave me a shy smile and said quietly, "I've begun dating again."

I don't know what impossible situation you might be facing right now, but I do know that when you add a little bit of faith to a little bit of action, miracles still happen. Hope is reborn, relationships are healed, debts get eliminated, people find lifelong mates, an impossible neighbor becomes interested in faith, dying churches turn a corner, classes get passed, books get written, and life is worth living again.

So what's your tangled mess of barbed wire? And where do you need to start moving and tugging? What's the one thing you want to overcome that feels overwhelming? No matter what you are facing, you can start tugging: you can fast and pray, assess the condition, take ownership, and start moving.

It's one piece of barbed wire at a time.

8

Try Things You Can't Do

Stretch Yourself

Writing a book scares me to death. The thought of starting with an empty computer screen and filling it with 220 pages of original, God-inspiring material is terrifying. But then I read Henry Cloud's words in his book *Integrity*: "In order to grow you must attempt things you are unable to do."[1] I looked up from the page and thought, "What is it that I would like to do but can't do or have never tried to do?

One of those things for me is writing a book. For years I've dreamed of it, but then, *who am I to write a book? I'm not smart enough, creative enough, or talented enough*, and I convinced myself that I had nothing to offer. But then I read Cloud's words:

> People who grow jump in over their head. They try things that they cannot do, then stretch to become able to do what they are attempting. In fact, for growth to occur the attempt has to be about something that you are not able to do. It has

157

to be a try. . . . When people get married for the first time, for example, it's something they've never before attempted. By definition they don't know how to make it work. But, the having to make it work pushes them to grow.[2]

It's the same with dating for the first time, going to college, writing a paper, becoming a parent, teaching a class, or running a business. At some point all these things have to be a "try," because we've never attempted them before. And when we try something we can't do, we go through a process of stretching, failing, recalibrating, trying again, learning from mistakes, and growing stronger. Cloud says, "People who grow place themselves in situations that demand more of them than they are able to deliver."[3] Great words. I wish I'd written those words; people who write books write words like that. So I want to ask, "What is it in your life that you want to do but have convinced yourself you can't?"

Writing a book would have to be a "try" for me. So with a lot of uncertainty and insecurity, I loaded up my Ford Explorer with my books, laptop, notepads, two plastic bins full of stories, clippings, and messages; I packed my cooler with food and tossed in my bicycle, hip boots, and fishing gear. I was going up to a beautiful beach house near Bayfield, Wisconsin, on Lake Superior that some friends were letting me use. It was June, but a cold rain was blowing off the lake, and when I stopped to get gas south of Duluth, I almost froze to death; it was forty-one degrees. I have a hard time leaving my family and home whenever I go off by myself for a few days, but it's good whenever I do it because God always speaks to me by his Spirit and reveals things to me that I never notice when I'm in my daily work routine. But I get lonely, and the gloomy, cold day up north wasn't helping.

I continued on toward Bayfield, and after driving eight miles past it, I finally located the place where I'd be staying. I'd never been there before, I was two hundred miles away from home, and I was relieved to find the key under the mat.

But when I opened the front door, I saw that the entire first floor was flooded with two inches of sewage water. I was so stunned that it took me a few seconds to realize that this was real—and a major problem. I dropped my bags on the porch and tried to call the owners on my cell phone, but there was no service in this remote little town. So I rolled up my pant legs and sloshed my way through the hallway and into the living room looking for where the water was coming from. I found the bathroom and saw that the toilet was running. It had been running for three days and had filled their three-thousand-gallon septic tank. The system was completely backed up, and the stuff was now coming up through the drains in the showers and from who knows where else.

So I sloshed my way back through the living room and into the kitchen looking for the phone; no phone in the kitchen. My shoes were completely soaked, and I didn't want to keep making waves through the living room, splashing water onto the leather-backed sofas, but I had to find a phone. No phone in the living room. I walked up their beautifully finished cedar staircase with water squishing out of my shoes, but the cordless phone upstairs didn't work. I frantically went back downstairs and finally found the main phone sitting behind a couch; it was under water, so that phone didn't work. Now what? I drove back into town, pulled up to a small-engine repair shop, and said, "I've got a minor emergency here. Could I please use your phone?" I got in touch with my friends and explained the situation. They made a call and then called me back to tell me that the septic service would be there in an hour.

Two hours later Septic Jim showed up wearing knee-high rubber boots, black rubber gloves, a mustache, and long, wet hair tucked under a hooded sweatshirt. His lack of any sort of smile or greeting let me know he wasn't thrilled about being there. And I've heard foul language before, but Septic Jim cussed like a Lake Superior sailor. Turns out he had sliced his hand open earlier in the day while working on a car and hadn't been to the doctor yet to get it stitched up, so the last thing he wanted to do was suck sewage. But he emptied the septic tank, and then we dragged about fifty feet of hose up to the house and into the kitchen. Septic Jim said to me, "I'll hold the *bleepin'* hose while you take the *bleepin'* squeegee and push the *bleepin'* water my way." I didn't have the heart to tell him I was a pastor—I figured he'd had enough bad news for one day. Septic Jim and I spent the next five hours sucking up sewage, moving furniture, and pulling out rugs. That was my first day of writing a book.

It's always a little creepy for me the first night when I'm staying all alone in somebody else's place, and with the cold rain and wet feet, I couldn't help wondering if God was trying to tell me something. What are the odds that I'd be given the keys to a beautiful home in which to work, only to find it flooded with sewage water? That's not a good sign by anyone's measure. But maybe God was giving me a gift and hitting me over the head with a fresh example of how true the subject matter of this book really is. I also remembered what Erwin McManus said about being in the center of God's will. He said, "Being in the center of God's will is not the safest place to be, it's often the most dangerous place to be."⁴ I would add that it's also sometimes the *smelliest* place to be.

More Water

When I think of someone who tried things he couldn't do and who put himself in situations that demanded more of him than he was able to deliver, I think of Joshua. Joshua lived during a time in Jewish history when the Israelites were trying to establish themselves as a new nation in the land of Canaan. Moses had led the Israelites out of captivity in Egypt, and after forty years of wandering through the desert, Moses brought them right up to the border of their new land. But

Moses was 120 years old, and his days on earth were coming to an end. So God told Moses to hand over the reigns of leadership to Joshua, and Joshua was commissioned by God and Moses to lead the people into their new land, fulfilling God's eternal promise. The Bible says, "Now Joshua son of Nun was filled with the Spirit of wisdom because Moses had laid his hands on him. So the Israelites listened to him and did what the LORD had commanded" (Deut. 34:9). Then God gave Joshua his full blessing when he said to him:

> Now . . . get ready to cross the Jordan River into the land I am about to give to them—to the Israelites. I will give you every place where you set your foot, as I promised Moses. Your territory will extend from the desert and from Lebanon to the great river, the Euphrates—all the Hittite country—and to the Great Sea on the west. No one will be able to stand up against you all the days of your life. As I was with Moses, so I will be with you; I will never leave you or forsake you. (Josh. 1:2–5)

What a send-off. God says he's going to give Joshua every place where he sets his foot, that no one will be able to stand against him, and that God will always be with him. Those are words of blessing and protection. You would think that when God makes a promise like that, he would make it easy for Joshua with no problems, setbacks, or resistance. The Israelites had just come through forty years of traveling like homeless people in the Sinai Desert; they could assume that it was time to reap the rewards that God promised them many years ago.

But instead, the first thing they encounter is water, lots of it, not from a backed-up septic tank but from a swollen Jordan River that's at flood stage. This was a real danger, a real threat to the Israelites, who were made up of six hundred thousand men, women, and children of all ages, with all their possessions, goods, and livestock. The Jordan River separated the people from the Promised Land, and it represented a real

161

problem for Israel. It's what stood between them and the life God had promised.

The Jordan actually starts up in Mount Hermon and flows down to the Sea of Galilee and then keeps flowing to the Dead Sea. Mount Hermon has an elevation of nine thousand feet, but the Dead Sea is thirteen hundred feet below sea level, so the river descends rapidly, making it difficult to cross, especially at flood stage. Joshua 3:15 says, "The Jordan is at flood stage all during harvest." Rivers at flood stage are very dangerous, with life-threatening undercurrents and speed. Originally the Jordan ran through a gorge called the Zor; the gorge was 150 feet wide and had steep banks that were twenty to thirty feet high. So when the Jordan was at flood stage, the entire gorge became filled with fast-moving water, and because the banks went straight up and down, if you went into the water, you went *into* the water and were likely swept away by the current, never to be seen again.

> If you are following God by faith, every once in awhile he will lead you to . . . a moment . . . where he will call you to take a step and try something you can't do.

That's important, because in Joshua 3:6 it says that Joshua turned to the priests and said, "Take up the ark of the covenant and pass on ahead of the people."

Imagine for a moment that you were one of the priests who was carrying the ark of the covenant, which was like carrying a millstone around your neck, and Joshua says to you, "I want you to be the first one to step into the Jordan River." If the river doesn't miraculously part or dry up, you're a goner. If I was the lead guy, I'd be tempted to fake a hamstring injury and sit this one out.

Joshua is asking the priests to do something they cannot do; he's asking them to do something that's impossible, that's beyond human reason or ability. Have you ever sensed God leading you to try something that's impossible? Thankfully, these into-the-river moments don't happen every day; most days are fairly routine and regular, nothing spectacular. But if you are following God by faith, every once in a while he will lead you to a river, to a moment, to a crossroad where he will call you to take a step and try something you can't do. And if you follow him, you will discover three huge payoffs.

First Payoff: You Experience God's Power

When you try things *you* can't do, you get a chance to see what *God* can do; you get to see God's miraculous power take over. God said to Joshua, "I want you to take the first step." Taking the first step into something you can't do is always the hardest step, and it requires complete trust in the power and goodness of God.

But think about it: stepping into something you can't do is the only time you *need* God's power.

If you never step into something you can't do, God's power isn't needed; and where God's power isn't needed, God's power doesn't show up. So I would ask you, "What river might you need to step into in order to see and experience God's power?" What is it that you can't do? What is it that you would like to do but you're afraid to try? If it's something God has put in your heart and it's gnawing and tugging at you and won't go away, that might be God's Spirit urging you to take the first step.

God can't take that step for you; you have to do what only *you* can do so that God can do what only *he* can do.

"But what if I can't do it, what if I fail, what if I look like a fool, what if God doesn't pull me through?" I have to fight through the "what ifs" every time I'm attempting to try something I can't do, even when I'm convinced that God is urging and calling me to do it.

Some people rarely experience God's power because they seldom attempt to accomplish something that would *require* his power. "God, give me lots of money *first*, then I'll be generous." Where's the miracle in that? There's no faith in that. "God, make my friend apologize to me first, then I'll forgive her." Or "God, make me a gifted, eloquent teacher, then I'll try to lead a class." Where's the need for God in that?

Now I do believe that people need to play to their strengths and step into areas in which they are gifted, but I also believe that there are times in your life when God will ask you to cross a Jordan River that is beyond your ability or area of expertise. God might prompt you to go back to school, stay home to raise your kids, extend forgiveness to someone who offended you, end a hurtful relationship, start a business, confront a family member, or give generously toward God's purposes, and everything in you might be telling you that you can't do it. And you're right. You can't. But if God is prompting and leading you, and if God has led you to a place where you will absolutely fail unless he shows up, will you trust him enough to take the first step so that he can show you his miraculous power? Paul, author of several books in the New Testament, said, "I will rejoice in my weaknesses, because when I am weak, then I am strong" (see 2 Cor. 12:9–10). When I'm at my weakest point, that's when I'm at my strongest point, because that's when I have to rely on God's power to do something amazing. Joshua said to the priests, "Take up the ark of the covenant and cross over ahead of the people." And I love the very next sentence: "So they took it up and went ahead of them" (Josh. 3:6). Flat out obedience. No arguing, no questioning. "So they took it up and went ahead of them."

At some point you just have to go.

If you ever want to experience God's power, you have to take a step and let the chips fall.

Some people spend their entire life standing on the banks of the Jordan waiting for a miracle to happen. Can I be lovingly direct? *Miracles never happen while you're standing safely on the river's edge; miracles happen only when you step into the unknown and impossible.* And this is true of all great people of faith and accomplishment. When God called Abraham, the Bible says, "Abraham . . . went, even though he did not know where he was going" (Heb. 11:8). When Jesus called Peter, it says, "So Peter went over the side of the boat" (Matt. 14:29 NLT). When Jesus called the first disciples, it says, "At once they left their nets and followed him" (Matt. 4:20).

Joshua told the priests to step into the Jordan with the ark and lead the way. "So they took it up and went ahead of them." At some point you have to stop thinking and start stepping, because nothing amazing ever happens while you're standing safely on the shore.

Every spring the walleyes and saugers (which are like walleyes) pile up below the dams and power plants on the Mississippi River near Red Wing, Minnesota. And if you hit it right, you can just hammer the saugers. So about sixteen years ago, I took my son, David, who was only six at the time, and we joined Mark Kalb, who's a pastor friend in Red Wing. We fished hard all morning up and down the river but didn't catch a thing. Not a bite, nibble, nothing.

By early afternoon Dave had had it. He said things like, "Dad, I'm bored; there aren't any fish in the river; when can we go home?" And because I was with my friend and didn't want to cut short his day of fishing, I was looking for anything to keep David occupied. We'd already burned through our lunch and snacks. Suddenly, four big mallard ducks set their wings and landed about twenty feet from our boat. They were wild ducks, but it was obvious they were used to getting handouts from fishermen, because they floated in close to our boat. I thought, "This is a godsend."

So I said to Dave, "Toss 'em some chips." Sure enough, they swam right up to the boat, grabbed a chip, and fluttered away. That kept Dave occupied for, oh, about a minute. Soon he was moaning and groaning about going home again. Mark and I were standing on the front of his bass boat talking about life, so just as a brush-off I said, "Dave, why don't you see if you can grab one?" knowing that it's impossible for *anyone* to grab a wild duck, much less a six-year-old kid.

But his eyes lit up. "Really, Dad?"

"Sure, Dave, knock yourself out."

So with a whole new purpose, he rolled up his sleeves and started throwing out more chips. You've heard of oil slicks—this was a "chip slick." Mark and I weren't paying much attention to him. We were standing on the front of the boat, and all the while Dave was hanging over the back, and all we could see was his rear end. Then all of a sudden we heard David yell, "Dad, I got one!" Mark and I looked up just in time to see David fall into the boat with his hands clutched around the neck of a huge mallard duck. Its wings were whacking and flapping and slapping him in the face right and left. Dave was taking a beating from this bird that was almost as big as he was because he had his little grubby hands clutched around its neck.

He was lying on his back on the bottom of the boat with this bird just beating the heck out of him. Finally, he yelled, "Dad, what should I do?"

I yelled back, "Dave, let him go!" So he released his grip, and that huge bird flew off, wondering what had just happened. David stood to his feet, all wet and shook up, and Mark and I doubled over in laughter.

Finally, after the commotion settled down, I said, "Dave, how did you ever do that?"

He said, "Well, when I tossed in a chip, it would sink down a little bit, and the ducks would put their head under water to grab it, and I thought, 'That's a good time,' so I went," and he made a fast downward motion with his hand and said, "I grabbed one, like that."

I said, "That's brilliant!" I proudly turned to Mark and said, "That's *my* boy!" That's the day we went fishing and caught a duck, and it was the most amazing, most memorable fishing trip I've ever had.

But what I love about that story is David's childlike faith. The son hears his father say, "Why don't you try to catch a duck." And it's completely impossible; it's something that nobody can do, especially a six-year-old little boy. But because he trusts his dad, he rolls up his sleeves and gives it a whirl, because nothing ever happens if you don't try.

When you try things you can't do, you get a chance to see what *God* can do. Joshua 3:15–17 says, "The Jordan is at flood stage all during harvest. Yet as soon as the priests who carried the ark reached the Jordan and their feet touched the water's edge, the water from upstream stopped flowing. It piled up in a heap . . . [and] was completely cut off. . . . The priests who carried the ark of the covenant of the LORD stood firm on dry ground in the middle of the Jordan, . . . until the whole nation had completed the crossing on dry ground." The first payoff when you try things you can't do: you get a chance to see what God can do.

Second Payoff: You Expand Your Capacity to Tackle Greater Challenges

When you attempt things you can't do, you grow new muscles to take on bigger challenges. In Joshua 3:10, Joshua said to the Israelites, "This is how you will know that the living God is among you, and that he will certainly drive out before you the Canaanites, Hittites, Hivites, Perizzites, Girgashites, Amorites and Jebusites." Joshua is saying that crossing the Jordan is the least of their problems. There are at least seven enemy nations waiting to go to war against them as soon as they cross the river. But Joshua says that this first step into the Jordan will expand their capacity to face greater challenges. When the Israelites see how God provides a way through the river by holding back the water, then they will know "that the living God is among them," and they will be emboldened to take on greater challenges.

Ten years ago we voted to add a two-million-dollar children's wing to our original campus, and I remember feeling overwhelmed and insecure about what seemed to me an insurmountable amount of money. It was three times our annual budget, but we were growing rapidly and were in dire need of children's space. I remember walking around the newly poured footings and watching the walls go up and wondering how we were ever going to pay for it.

Two years later we voted to build a new four-million-dollar worship center, and again I thought we were stepping way beyond our financial capabilities. But we had managed to pay off the children's wing, and so I thought, "Well, God provided for that; maybe God will provide for this." Before the worship center was finished, everybody knew it was too small. As soon as it opened, we filled it four times every weekend, and we could see that God was blessing our steps into the river.

Then three years later we voted to buy one hundred acres and build a new campus for twenty-seven million dollars—an insane, impossible challenge. But we sensed that God was prompting us, leading us, and compelling us to go. There were some voices telling us to cap our growth, plant smaller daughter churches, and stand safely by the river's edge. These voices were urging us to do what was doable, but rarely had God asked us to do what was doable. He always asked us to do what was *not* doable so that we would get a chance to see God's power. This would be a step into the unknown that would certainly fail if God didn't show up and provide a way.

And we would never have had the courage to take that impossible step had God not expanded our capacity by taking us through smaller rivers first. We've been in our new building for three years, and we have grown from two thousand people ten years ago to four thousand, six thousand, eight thousand, thirteen thousand people. We added a third campus, and then a fourth, and now are planning a fifth. And none of it would have happened had we not taken that first step into the Jordan River with our children's wing. Joshua told the Israelites that when the priests take that first step and they see how God will part the river, then they will know that God is with them, and it will embolden them to take on greater challenges that lie ahead.

Gary Haugen is the president of International Justice Mission. He's a Harvard-educated lawyer who started out working for the US Department of Justice as the senior trial attorney. Gary could be living a safe, cushy life somewhere, but he's chosen to use his experience and skills to go into the dirtiest, darkest corners of the globe and work with often corrupt legal systems to free children who are bought and sold in the sex trade. He's rescued little boys and girls as young as eight years old who've been forced into a lifestyle of system-ized rape for profit, who endure ongoing sexual assault in the back rooms of brothels. Gary met with our leadership team for a couple hours a few months ago and said:

> What we do is dangerous, and it scares me. I've had co-workers shot and murdered for trying to close down these sex rings. I *want* to be brave, but I also want to be safe; I want to be brave *and* safe. But that's not possible. I can't be brave and safe; it has to be one or the other. And I think God calls us entirely not to be safe. Who's going to intervene for those who don't have a voice, who don't have protection, who get preyed upon simply because they can't defend themselves?
>
> Choosing this line of work is not safe! But I have found that when I am safe, I don't pray as much or rely on God as much. How many of us have taken on challenges that we can't imagine doing without prayer? Get involved in something that is not safe, and your devotional life will catch fire. Most people do devotions because they think they have to, not because they're at the end of their rope, in trouble and out on a limb. But if you start attempting things that are not safe, you will find yourself praying because you'll collapse in fear if you don't; you'll find yourself praying because you're in trouble if God doesn't show up. You'll find yourself reading the Bible not out of duty but because if you don't have God's wisdom it could cost people their lives; you read God's

Word because you have to know what God says in order to get out alive. God has called us to be brave, and that means we must increasingly live lives that are not safe.

When was the last time you and I chose to step into something that was not safe? When was the last time we *had* to pray and *had* to read God's Word because we'd collapse in fear if we didn't? Most of us live lives that are entirely too safe, standing on the banks of the river wondering why God doesn't do something amazing. In order to see and experience God's power, you have to give yourself to something that is not safe, and if you do, you will become a bigger, bolder person.

> In order to see and experience God's power, you have to give yourself to something that is not safe, and if you do, you will become a bigger, bolder person.

One of the reasons I like to tackle tough challenges is because it stretches my capacity. I'm a buck-fifty drippin' wet. I'm not a big person, but I subject my skinny, little body to the rigors and extremes of the Hog Hole trip every year because they expand my capacity to face other challenges. The demands of that trip force me to stay physically and mentally fit; they push me to my absolute limits. Many times we stagger to the finish line, sometimes in a downpour with bloodied knuckles and burning muscles, and we drop our packs and canoes in the sand and just hug each other in exhaustion and elation. It's a beautiful feeling, because it makes me feel like a bolder person. It's a test of character and strength that I can't get by sitting at a desk or playing golf, because it requires more of me than I have; it keeps me edgy and unsafe, and it increases my capacity to try things I can't do. Then when I'm faced with challenges like raising several million dollars, or giving a scary amount of money to a worthy cause, or asking forgiveness, or going to counseling, or dealing with deacons, they seem less formidable because I've conditioned myself to face much tougher challenges.

Joshua was saying that if they succeeded at crossing the Jordan, they would gain the courage and capacity to fight the enemy. When you try things you can't do, when you're unsafe, when you require more of yourself than you have, you give God a chance to show up and do something amazing. And it increases your capacity and courage to tackle even greater challenges.

Third Payoff: It Inspires Others to Try Things They Can't Do

When you try bold things, others will be inspired to do the same. The Israelites had crossed the Jordan River, and they were standing on the new land God had promised them. Joshua 4:18 says, "No sooner had they set their feet on the dry ground than the waters of the Jordan returned to . . . flood stage as before." But before that miracle occurred, Joshua instructed twelve men from the twelve tribes of Israel to take twelve large stones from the middle of the Jordan, where the priests had stood, and they built a memorial representing the twelve tribes of Israel. Joshua 4:6–7 says, "[This memorial] will serve as a sign among you. In the future, when your children ask you, 'What do these stones mean?' tell them that the flow of the Jordan was cut off before the ark of the covenant of the LORD. . . . These stones are to be a memorial to the people of Israel forever." Joshua 4 concludes with these words: "The LORD your God dried up the Jordan before you until you had crossed over. . . . He did this so that all the peoples of the earth might know that the hand of the LORD is powerful and so that you might always fear the LORD your God" (vv. 23–24).

"All the peoples of the earth" is a reference to you and to me. God did this so that *we* would remember that God is still involved in our lives, is still powerful, is still able and willing to help us do things we can't do ourselves. Joshua instructed the twelve men to erect a memorial so that their children would always remember that God is capable of doing miracles and so that they'd be inspired to follow God into unknown and impossible adventures. They erected a memorial so that *all the peoples of the earth* (you and me) would know that God is powerful and so that we'd be inspired to try things we can't do so that we'd get a chance to see what God can do.

I love to be inspired, and I need to be inspired, because I lose my courage so quickly. And I quickly forget the miracles that God has performed all through my life. I forget. Dozens of times I've made my lunch and left it sitting in plain sight on the counter as I've walked out the door. A couple years ago I signed and dated my Alaska fishing license July 28, 1999; it was 2009. I forget entire decades—they should never let me lead a church or write sermons. So I need other people to regularly inspire me and remind me of all the amazing ways God has led me and wants to continue to use me.

One Sunday afternoon in June 2008, I watched the final championship tennis match at Wimbledon between Spaniard Rafael Nadal and Swiss Roger Federer. It was the longest final match in Wimbledon's 133-year history: four hours and forty-eight minutes—more than seven hours with rain delays. The youngster, Nadal, pulled ahead two sets to none and was serving for the match in the third set when a rain delay interrupted play. When the players returned, Federer, who had won sixty-five straight matches on grass, dug deep and held off Nadal and won the third and forth sets. The fifth and final set went to four/four, five/five, six/six, and was finally won by Nadal, eight/six, just before the match was called due to darkness. They were like two prizefighters who took blow after blow and wouldn't fall.

I was watching the final half hour while exercising on an elliptical machine at the health club—I had eight minutes to go on a thirty-minute workout, and my whole body hurt.

My muscles were burning, I felt faint, my shirt was soaked, and I wanted to step down and quit. But I was watching this amazing match, and I was so inspired by their relentless will to win that there was no way I could quit. I told myself, "Suck it up, Merritt. Don't be such a pansy. Grind it out and finish it off. These two champions battled for four hours and forty-eight minutes; the least you can do is finish your thirty-minute workout." When I see other people trying things they can't do, it inspires me to try things I can't do.

I was inspired one night twelve years ago, and it was completely unexpected. My daughter spent thousands of hours practicing six days a week for ten years in the sport of gymnastics, which meant that I spent countless hours drifting aimlessly down school hallways between Megan's four events looking at photographs, trophies, and high school memorabilia. She'd do a thirty-second bar routine, and then it was a forty-five-minute wait until her five-second vault; she'd do her five-second vault, and then it was a forty-five-minute wait until her twenty-second beam routine. This happened at every four-hour-long meet. Gymnastics is inspiring for a total of one minute and thirty-five seconds.

But I have a memory that will always inspire me to try things I can't do, and it happened unexpectedly. Our daughter was selected to attend an awards banquet at the Regal Hotel in Minneapolis to honor a dozen gymnasts from the state of Minnesota for their achievements. The University of Minnesota women's gymnastic team was there, along with their coaches. And John Roethlisberger, who is a two-time Olympian and the most decorated athlete in the history of the University of Minnesota, was also there. One by one these twelve kids were called to the front by this world-renowned athlete, and as they came forward to receive their award, John would announce two or three of their achievements. Then he'd conclude with that gymnast's most outstanding achievement: "first in state," or "went to regionals," or "went to nationals," and everybody would applaud.

173

But as we sat there, I noticed a young girl sitting with her family about three tables in front of us. It was obvious that she was mentally and physically challenged. She would wave at odd times, clap and speak out at odd times, and I figured she was there to watch a sister or brother receive an award.

But when John announced the final gymnast, he mentioned that this particular gymnast had made the special gymnastic team at her school. He mentioned a few other minor achievements, and then he paused. And before he called her to the platform to receive her award and stand with all the other gymnasts, John Roethlisberger, this great Olympian, looked down at Julie and said, "And Julie's most outstanding achievement *was learning how to walk independently.*" With great effort she stood to her feet. Her smile was brighter than the chandeliers above her. Her dad stood to assist her, he walked with her a few steps, and then he let her go. And with a shuffle and a limp, Julie walked proudly all by herself to receive her award from John, and everyone in the room stood to their feet in spontaneous applause.

It inspired me; it continues to inspire me. As I watched her, I wondered what kind of impossible rivers Julie had to cross to get to this proud moment in her life. She would never do a backflip off the beam, she would never represent her team at state, but she could walk independently, and it was her most outstanding achievement.

I have faced many challenges in life, but I have never had to relearn how to walk independently. I take walking for granted, and running, working, writing, creating, and leading. When I see people like Julie step into impossible rivers like learning how to walk independently with limited resources, I wonder what I should be capable of doing with my unlimited resources. Whenever I see brave souls overcome impossible barriers, I am inspired to try even greater things that I can't do. In Luke 12:48, Jesus said, "To whom much is given, much is required" (author paraphrase). That's me. And that's most of you.

■Three Cautions

Make Sure God Is Leading You

Deuteronomy 34:9 says, "Now Joshua son of Nun was *filled with the Spirit of wisdom* because Moses had laid his hands on him." Joshua was filled with the Spirit of wisdom, which means that Joshua was getting an ongoing supply of discernment that came directly from God's Holy Spirit. All through Old Testament history, God would select a leader like Moses or Joshua and would supply them with an on-going stream of wisdom and direction so that they could instruct and lead the people. The Bible, God's Word, hadn't yet been written, and Jesus hadn't yet come, so the primary way God revealed truth and wisdom to people was by his Holy Spirit.

Sometimes God's Spirit would reveal things through dreams, visions, or an angelic being. One time God used the voice of a donkey to reveal his truth, another time a burning bush. But God usually revealed his truth and purposes in the way he did it with Joshua: *by filling Joshua with wisdom that came from the Holy Spirit.* It wasn't something Joshua could explain, predict, or manufacture, but when it happened, Joshua couldn't keep it bottled inside. The leading from God's Spirit was so strong that he *knew* it was from God. But just to confirm it, God told Joshua, "Today I will begin to exalt you in the eyes of all Israel, so they may know that I am with you as I was with Moses. Tell the priests who carry the ark of the covenant . . . [to] go and stand in the river" (Josh. 3:7–8). God let Joshua and all the people know that God's Spirit was leading Joshua by miraculously stopping the river. They'd seen God hold back waters once before, forty years prior when Moses led the Israelites across the Red Sea, and now they would see it again.

Whenever I feel prompted to try something I can't do, I try to make sure it is God who is leading me and not just human desire. I look for four signals. First, do I sense an inner prompting or an inner tug on my heart from God's Spirit? Every time I've been led by God, it began with an unmistakable prompting that wouldn't go away. Second, does it line up with Scripture? I know, for example, that if I feel compelled to do something that's immoral, would harm my family, or would weaken the church, it can't be God's leading, because those things are in conflict with Scripture. Third, do other wise and godly people agree with it, and have I sought their counsel? If everyone whom I trust disagrees, that's a red flag. Fourth, do the circumstances make sense: Is the opportunity there, is the timing right, does it seem like the circumstances are pointing in that direction?

Make sure God is leading you.

Be Realistic

Be as prepared as you can be before you try something you can't do. Consider your background, experience, skills, and training, because there's a difference between *realistic* steps of faith and *foolish* steps of faith. God will ask us to do things we can't do, but it's not blind faith or stupid faith. I am 99 percent sure that God is not calling any of you to Nome, Alaska, to start a business in ceramic figurines. That's not realistic; that's foolishness. There's a difference between realistic risk and foolish risk. Gary Haugen of the International Justice Mission doesn't go into dangerous hot spots haphazardly; he builds alliances, marshals his resources, considers the timing, and brings more than twenty years of expertise. And *then* he tries things he can't do.

Expect Problems

You'd think that when you obey God's leading, everything would go smoothly, but it seldom does. As soon as the Israelites cross the Jordan River into the Promised Land, they are met with war, and they have to take out the cities of Jericho and Ai. Problems.

They conquered Jericho, but Joshua's men disobeyed his orders and kept some of the plunder for themselves instead of putting it all into the corporate treasury. So Scripture says, "The LORD's anger burned against Israel" (Josh. 7:1). Consequently, when they went up against the city of Ai, God removed his protection, and they got beaten badly. More problems.

God was giving them this land, but Joshua had to launch dozens of military campaigns against the Hittities, Amorites, Canaanites, Perizzites, Hivites, Jebusites, and Philistines. It seemed that Israel's bold step of faith ended up causing nothing but problems.

Do you ever feel like your life is one big problem?

We all know what it's like to have problems. You sense God leading you to try something you can't do, and you take a bold step into the unknown. At first it's thrilling, but then there's a series of conflicts, heartbreaks, and obstacles, and it's easy to fall facedown and lose heart. You are led into a new position at work only to be undermined and criticized. You are led to go back to school only to run into stressful classes. You are led to start giving generously only to have your car break down. You are led to write a book only to have an editor cut, criticize, and make you redo your work. And because of the threat of conflict and failure, some people play it safe; consequently, their life never changes. Anyone who attempts to try things they can't do will encounter problems. Those problems aren't there to stop you but to embolden you. They're there to show you that God is there, his power is real, and it is available to those who will take the step. Problems are opportunities for God's power. No problems, no power.

People who never cross the Jordan might avoid some conflict and hardship, but they never see new land, they seldom grow, and they rarely experience the thrill of following God into the unknown and watching him do impossible things.

I wonder how many unfulfilled dreams there are in people who are still standing at the river's edge, how many unresolved conflicts, unexplored adventures, untaught courses, unused talents. Henry Cloud talks about people who live their lives in a "dull state of sameness." He writes, "You could peer into their lives year after year and see that there's no difference in the way they relate to their spouse, kids, coworkers and careers *just following the conveyer belt of sameness.*"[5]

> If you want to see God do amazing things in your life . . . then you eventually have to step into the river.

If you want to see God do amazing things in your life, and if you want to expand your capacity to face greater challenges, then you eventually have to step into the river and try things you can't do.

You might fail, you might become afraid, you might have to go through some battles, but you might achieve something that was far beyond your dreams or abilities. That's when life gets exciting.

At one time I was unable to do many of the things I can do now, like write a message, give a speech, fix a washing machine, create a lesson plan, teach a class, manage a staff, filet a fish, be a husband, raise two kids, lead a church. Every one of those things required that I try things I couldn't do. So step into the river, get your feet wet, try something you can't do, and maybe God will do a miracle and show you what *he* can do.

How will you ever know unless you try?

9

Avoid the Fatal Fall

Practice Self-Control

It was late August, and after sleeping on the hard ground all night, I sat up in my sleeping bag and tried to unkink my sore body. I located my pants at the bottom of the tent and slid them over my chicken legs. I poked my head out of my tent to the fog rising off Crooked Lake in the early dawn; the cold morning air sent a chill through my body. We were seventeen miles from nowhere in the most remote part of the Boundary Waters Canoe Area (BWCA). It was day one in the Hog Hole, and I couldn't wait to start a fire and get the coffee going.

This is a hard and dangerous trip, and we take every precaution. Every year people die in the BWCA from hypothermia or drowning; others are badly injured from ankle breaks, cuts, and gashes. Bears are always a concern, but the water is what scares me the most, and canoes aren't the most stable vessels. The dark, tinted water never really warms up—in late

August the water temperature drops to the low fifties—and there's a spooky undercurrent that must always be respected.

In twenty-five trips or so, we'd had only minor mishaps, until that August morning 2005. Oz Larsen and Chris Whachler were with me—both experienced canoeists and woodsmen. We had invited a fourth person on this trip, Dean Hager, who'd never paddled a canoe and knew nothing about the BWCA. As a rule, we don't bring rookies into the Hole, because we like coming out alive. But Dean's a good friend and always up for an adventure. He's also a triathlete, so he's strong; a high-level executive at a large software company, so he's smart; our church chairman, so he's a leader; and a father of three little girls, so he's outnumbered at home and needed a break. Dean was a good risk, or so I thought.

At 6:15 a.m. on that first morning, I slipped on a sweatshirt and a wool stocking hat; I could see my breath. I crawled out of the tent, and there was Dean standing on a rock, shivering and wearing only his swim trunks and goggles. He pointed across the water and said, "Is that an island?"

"That's a big island," I told him. "Maybe a mile all the way around it." I said sternly, "Why don't you wait for it to warm up, Dean? Wait until midday when we can paddle alongside you."

Twice I warned him not to go, and he hesitated, but I could see it in his eyes, and I know the personality—determined and driven. He said, "I'll just swim across the channel, and if I feel okay, I'll keep going around the island. Be back in a half hour or so." I started gathering wood for the fire as I watched Dean swim away.

Ten minutes later Oz crawled out of his tent just in time to see Dean disappear around the corner of the island. Oz said, "He's nuts."

Chris crawled out next and said, "He's nuts."

The three of us muddled around the campsite getting breakfast ready, checking on bait, unpacking our fishing gear—all of us casting an occasional glance at the channel to where Dean should've been rounding the bend at any second.

Twenty minutes later Oz said to Chris, "We better take your canoe to go check on him." Chris had just sat down against a tree with his coffee and said, "Let me finish my coffee first." Morning coffee in the Hog Hole is a sacred experience.

Jokingly I said, "He's *your* bowman, Chris; be a long paddle back without him." After Chris finished his coffee, he got up, and I could tell he was a little miffed that he had to go out and retrieve the rookie.

Chris and Oz slid their Kevlar Minnesota III into the water and headed in the opposite direction around the island to meet Dean. Fifteen minutes later I saw them coming around the other side, and they lifted their arms and hands toward me as if to say, "There's no sign of him." I gestured back with the same motion—no sign of Dean anywhere.

Chris and Oz rounded the island a second time. It had now been close to an hour, and my mind started racing: "How could Dean have missed the turn? I forgot to tell him about the shallow reef halfway around—maybe he had hit his head; maybe he was hypothermic." All of us were thinking about the real possibility that Dean could've drowned; he wouldn't be the first.

I dug some firecrackers out of my pack that I carry to scare off bears, and I ran down the shoreline blowing them off one by one, hoping the loud echo would give Dean a reference point. No response. There are hundreds of little ins and outs in the Boundary Waters, and the shorelines can blend together, making everything look the same.

Chris and Oz paddled back to the campsite to pick me up and grab some extra clothes and matches. A brooding silence hung between us. Finally, I said, "Let's face it, there are only two possibilities: either he's lost, or he drowned." Nobody responded.

We circled the island a third time, scanning the dark water for a body. An hour and a half had passed. I thought, "How long do we search? When do we paddle six hours back to Ely for a float plane? If he's lying on land somewhere, how much time before hypothermia sets in and his whole body shuts down? How will I face his wife, Jenny, and the girls? What about our church board, his company, *his funeral*. Why didn't I insist that he not go?" I felt sick to my stomach.

It was the first time the three of us had ever lost a friend like this, and our emotions ran from fear, to regret, to remorse, to utter disbelief. The thoughts I had of facing the moment when we found him are beyond description. As each half hour passed, our hope for a good outcome dwindled. Before he left the campsite, I remember Dean saying, "I'll keep the island on my left at all times; that way I won't get lost." Even though it looked as if there was no way he could've missed the turn up the channel that led to our campsite, we started thinking through all the possibilities, all the shoots, bays, and shorelines he could've taken.

One by one we eliminated the options, finally settling on one final possibility, one final hope. It had now been two hours. "Maybe he missed the turn, kept swimming down the shoreline, and turned into the next shoot . . ." We set out, paddled a mile or so past the channel that he should have come through, followed that shoreline, rounded the bend, and turned down the next shoot, which dead-ends two miles down. We paddled a hundred yards down the shoot and let the canoe drift to a stop. Nothing. In silence, we put our paddles in the water to turn around, when suddenly Oz said, "There he is!" Where? Was he on land, floating in the water? Oz said, "Way down there. He's waving his arms."

Chris and I looked up, and about a mile down the shoreline we could see a person that looked like a tiny speck. We hung our heads in relief. Dean had swum more than four miles in fifty-degree water. He was alive, but Chris wanted to kill him. So I said, "Give him a break, then we'll kill him." We paddled up to Dean, who was slapping his body trying to keep warm. He looked pale and shaken. I said, "Did you think this is Dead Moose Bay?" which is where our campsite was. Dean said, "I have no idea where I am." After two hours of swimming in ice-cold water, Dean had collapsed onto that rock. His feet were numb, and his body was shutting down. He'd begun hallucinating and thought he was seeing our campsite across from where he'd collapsed.

Dean came close to losing his life that day. He was able to clothe himself and stumble into the canoe. He apologized repeatedly and thanked us for not giving up on him. He wondered how he could ever make it up to us. I said, "Don't worry. You just became prime sermon material for about twelve thousand people. Might even show up in a book someday." A week later I received a handwritten note in the mail that was signed, "Thanks for not giving up, Dean."

The question is, why do really smart people sometimes do really dumb things? Dean knew the risks. I warned him twice, told him about the currents and about people who lose their lives every year in the Boundary Waters. Later he admitted to us that he's prone to getting lost. When he travels on business trips, Dean is famous for going for a run and not being able to find his hotel again. He once went on a half-hour run in Paris and found his hotel four hours later. The reason smart people do dumb things is not because they lack knowledge, information, or intelligence. Dean had all of that. It's something else.

Moral Falls

Move into the realm of sexual morality. Most of us could readily list really smart, often prominent, people who forfeited their career, marriage, family, and future for an affair or an illegal business move. Presidential candidate John Edwards is extremely intelligent and successful, a United States senator. Edwards had to know that having an affair during his 2008 campaign for the presidency would jeopardize his chances, if not eliminate them altogether. What was it that caused him to ignore all wisdom and intelligence and risk his chance for the presidency for a fling?

Ted Haggard, former pastor of New Life Church in Colorado Springs, was a rising star in the church world, appearing on media outlets like CNN, *Larry King Live*, FOX News, and *Oprah*. I used to watch him speak on TV and marvel at his charisma and ability. He and his church were in the national spotlight for their explosive growth and ministry impact. He'd written books and was the president of the National Association of Evangelicals. Ted Haggard preached against sexual immorality; he knew this stuff backward and forward. He's extremely intelligent and gifted and, I think in most areas of his life, moral. Ted Haggard knew that visiting a male prostitute, even if it was just for massages, was way out of bounds. He knew that kind of behavior would wreck his reputation and strip him of everything he'd accomplished. But he did it anyway. Thankfully, under new leadership, the church is regaining strength. But what was it that caused Ted Haggard to ignore all reason and intelligence and do irrevocable damage to himself, his marriage, his church, and his future?

I've had three close friends who went through seminary, were respected leaders in their churches, taught regularly against sexual immorality, yet took devastating falls in this area. In each case, I was blindsided when it became public knowledge—and it always becomes public knowledge. Each of them was able to save his marriage and gain some restoration in ministry, but the price he paid in lost time, friends, trust, and future opportunities was steep and ongoing. What was it that caused these three incredibly smart people to set aside their intelligence and go down a path of certain loss and regret?

Some are able to recover a portion of their former life, but not without deep losses and lifelong regrets. Tiger Woods will always be talented and wealthy; he'll win more golf tournaments. But what good is it if he loses his wife and children? Again, why do really smart people sometimes do really stupid, often career-ending, family-ending things?

It's not because they lack intelligence or even some degree of morality. There's something more, something that overrides intelligence.

Not surprisingly, the Bible gives us the answer. Fatal falls are not new to mankind; they started with *the* fall in the Garden of Eden. And we've been tripping and falling ever since.

A King's Fall

One of the most famous falls happened to Israel's most successful and intelligent leader. The Bible says that David became king when he was thirty years old and reigned over Israel for forty years (2 Sam. 5:4–5). David was a fierce warrior, the Braveheart of his day. In one campaign, the Bible says, "David captured a thousand . . . chariots, seven thousand charioteers and twenty thousand foot soldiers" (2 Sam. 8:4). When the enemy sent in reinforcements, "David struck down twenty-two thousand of them" (v. 5). The guy was a stud in battle.

He was also an intellect. He wrote some of history's most articulate and thoughtful prose. Next to Jesus's Lord's Prayer, David's Twenty-Third Psalm is perhaps the most widely quoted prose of all time. First Chronicles 18:14 says, "David reigned over all Israel, doing what was just and right for all his people." David knew right from wrong. He was a brilliant military strategist, a fierce warrior, an accomplished author and musician, and to top it all off, he did what was just and right for all his people. He was a good king, and he treated people fairly. David did the right things.

But one day, a day when David should've been on the battlefield leading his men, he got out of bed, and the Bible says, "David . . . walked around on the roof of his palace. From the roof he saw a woman bathing. The woman was very beautiful, and David sent someone to find out about her. The man said, 'Isn't this Bathsheba, the daughter of Eliam and the wife of Uriah the Hittite?' Then David sent messengers to get her" (2 Sam. 11:2–4).

Consider the pain and loss of that single, selfish decision.

Pain and loss to Bathsheba, a married woman, who would bear the shame and guilt of being forced to lay with another man and bear his illegitimate child. She would also bear the loss of her husband, Uriah, whom David arranged to have murdered to cover up his sin.

To Uriah, who was murdered to pave the way for David to marry Uriah's wife.

To David's family. The prophet Nathan said to David, "Why did you despise the word of the LORD by doing what was evil in his eyes? . . . Now, therefore, the sword will never depart from your house, because you despised me and took the wife of Uriah the Hittite to be your own" (2 Sam. 12:9–10).

The Bible says that sin always brings death—death to purity, innocence, and relationships. Death came to David and Bathsheba's newborn son. It came to David's son Amnon, who forced himself on his sister Tamar and as a result was murdered by his brother Absalom. Death came to Absalom, who ended up hating David, his own father, and was killed while trying to chase down and kill David. The price David paid for one careless choice was a never-ending wave of death and destruction to his family. David wrote in Psalm 38:17, "I am about to fall, and my pain is *ever* with me." Some falls are fatal, and the pain never goes away. Is there forgiveness and restoration? Yes, but not without lasting consequences.

So how could this incredibly intelligent and righteous man do something that was so stupid and wicked? It wasn't due to a lack of intelligence, and it wasn't because David was completely immoral. After all, Scripture says that "he did what was just and right." There was something else that made David vulnerable to a fall. It's the same thing that makes us vulnerable.

The Emotional "Want To"

The reason so many smart people are capable of committing life-altering blunders is because something overrides intellect and knowledge, and that something is emotion. When you allow yourself to get too close to something that you're attracted to, your emotions kick in, and the emotional "want to" becomes so strong that it overrides your ability to back off and say no. When push comes to shove, whether it's a financial, relational, or even recreational decision, emotion trumps intellect every time.

How many of us have set a specific dollar amount for the purchase of a car, home, boat, dress, or electronic gizmo that we vowed we would not exceed but ended up spending hundreds, even thousands, of dollars more? I have, and most of you have. Why? Because the emotion associated with newer, brighter, and better trumps all reason. We do it because our emotional "want to" overrides our intellect.

> Smart people are capable of commiting life-altering bluders because [emotion] overrides intellect and knowledge.

The apostle Paul is one of the heroes of the Christian faith, but even he admits, "I have the desire to do what is good, but I cannot carry it out" (Rom. 7:18). He knows what he should do, he even has the desire to do it, but he can't execute. What's his problem? He tells us a few verses later: "In my inner being I delight in God's law; but I see another law at work in the members of my body, waging war against the law of my mind" (vv. 7:22–23). In other words, he knows and agrees with what's right and good—*he delights in God's law*. But there's another "law" at work inside him, and this other "law" wages war against his mind, against what he *knows* to be right and true.

A few verses earlier Paul identifies this other "law" as "sinful passions" and "evil desires." Passions and desires are connected to our emotions, not our intellect. And this "law" is like a law of nature—it's there, it can't be altered or eradicated. Our passions and desires wage war against our mind or intellect. And if we allow them, they will override our intellect, which is why Paul says, "I have the desire to do what's good, but I cannot carry it out." It's why really smart people are capable of doing really dumb things. There's a point at which they get too close to the line, their passions and desires rise up, and their emotional "want to" overrides their intellect.

When my friend Dean stood on that rock at 6:15 a.m., he knew the water was cold, the current was strong, and the area was unfamiliar; he knew about his proclivity to get lost. But his "want to" was so strong and his desire to train for the triathlon had such a pull on him that he ignored his intellect and let his emotions override all common sense. And he almost paid the ultimate price.

So if Paul says, "I have the desire to do what's good, but I cannot carry it out," are we doomed? Is there no hope? There are three safeguards you can employ to prevent you from taking a fatal fall.

Know Your Vulnerabilities

Where are you weak? What stores, websites, images, people, or places trigger your passions and desires? People have vulnerabilities in the area of spending, eating, relating, and recreating. Take a moment and reflect on where you're most vulnerable. Determine where you are weak, because that's where you're most likely to take a fall. If you know where you're vulnerable, then you know what to guard against or avoid altogether.

Avoid Areas of Vulnerability

I do mentoring work with some Norwegian pastors and churches, so I've been to Oslo several times. One night I got to my hotel room late after traveling all day, I turned on the

TV, and as I was flipping through the channels I came across the Exotic Entertainment channel with a ten-second trailer that was about as raw as could be. This happens in most European hotel rooms. These channels entice hotel occupants to watch for about thirty dollars a day. All you have to do is enter your room number. Nobody knows, nobody sees; it's just you and the TV. And that's the moment of truth. That's the moment when your character is tested.

How will you decide? Will you enter your room number and subject yourself to something that'll violate your marriage, damage your mind, and start or feed an all-consuming addiction? Or will you quickly flip to CNN? In that split second, you have to use an inner strength that's been built up over time that overpowers enormous temptation; there has to be an ingrained response that enables you to immediately turn away. If you linger, if you contemplate, allowing your thoughts and emotions to drift toward that channel, you're doomed. Your emotions will override everything you know about the addictive, progressive nature of pornography, and you'll fall.

One of the ways I've learned to avoid this pitfall is to ask the front desk to remove all access to such channels before I get to my room. Not because my marriage is weak, because it's not. I have a great marriage. It's because of what I've observed—that really smart people who are devoted to their marriage and family cross this line all the time and suffer for it.

Sexual temptation is so insidious that I don't trust myself. When I see really smart people do really stupid things, I say, "Bob, note to self, smarter people than you have fallen." One of the pet phrases I've repeated to my kids, congregation, and myself is, "Never put yourself in a situation where something could happen." Don't put yourself in a situation where an emotion gets triggered, a spark gets lit, a line gets crossed.

Call me extreme, but I don't think colleagues of the opposite sex should ride alone in a car together, have lunch

189

alone, or meet in an office without first telling an assistant or colleague what's happening. I'd even make it a work policy. We had all our church offices built with a six-foot-high, one-foot-wide window by each door so that everything's visible and everyone's accountable. Several times I have stood before our staff of two hundred, drawn a single line down the middle of a whiteboard, and said, "Here's the line. Don't ever get near it."

If you're married and have a Facebook account, have you built in safeguards? A work colleague told me that she and her husband have agreed not to add former girlfriends or boyfriends as friends on Facebook. It starts out so innocently. Someone tries to "friend" you, or you're just "reconnecting with an old college friend." You might even innocently send them a message. Then they write back and suggest meeting for coffee. And if you happen to be in a place where things aren't the best at home, you're a prime candidate for a fall. Online can move off-line in a hurry.

The American Academy of Matrimonial Lawyers says 81 percent of its members have used or faced evidence plucked from Facebook, MySpace, and Twitter over the past five years.[1]

So don't put yourself in a situation where something could happen, because you and I are one touch, hug, note, email, lunch, kiss, emotion away from endless pain and regret. Don't even go near it. First Corinthians 6:18 says, "Flee from sexual immorality." Proverbs 4:14–15 says, "Do not set foot on the path of the wicked or walk in the way of evil men. Avoid it, do not travel on it; turn from it and go on your way." The best way to prevent your emotions from overriding your intellect is to avoid your areas of weakness. Don't get near them. Avoid them. Turn and walk away.

Whenever I talk about setting firm boundaries around relationships, I get emails criticizing me for being too rigid. People will say, "I have lunch dates and business appointments alone with people of the opposite sex all the time. These are some of my best friends." Certainly, whether you're married or single, it's good and healthy to have friendships with people of the opposite sex. I do as well.

But I've grown weary of sitting across the desk from highly intelligent people who let their friendship slip into an emotional or physical affair that wrecked their life. The reason we need to take every precaution is because there is a line that gets crossed by well-intended people all the time. They say, "I don't know how it happened." And they're right. They don't *know* how it happened, because it wasn't about knowing; it was about emotion. They crossed an invisible line where their emotions nullified their intellect. And once that line gets crossed, it's almost impossible to turn back. Not knowing where that line is should scare you into imposing some firm boundaries that you simply will not violate. You have way too much to lose. So do I.

Learn from Others' Mistakes

It amazes me how often I encounter people who are going along fine in life—have a decent job, a great spouse, wonderful kids, respect in the community—but then totally sink themselves by having an affair, stealing something from work, or getting arrested for a misdemeanor. Or I see teenagers who flunk out of school, get sexually careless, or form an addiction that puts them at an ongoing disadvantage. You don't have to wreck your life. It is possible to avoid the fatal falls that cause lifelong loss and regret.

One of the ways to avoid a fatal fall is to learn from others' mistakes. It doesn't take a person of great intelligence to watch someone hurl themselves off a cliff on a bicycle, see them crash and break numerous bones, to say, "Hmm, that looks really painful. I think I'll avoid that."

It doesn't take much intelligence to watch fellow students binge drink, puke all over themselves, engage in high-risk behaviors, miss class from hangovers, form an addiction, fail out of school, and end up in low-paying jobs to say, "Hmm, that looks really messed up. I think I'll avoid that."

It doesn't take super intelligence to watch people travel to a casino each weekend, blow their earnings, neglect their kids, form an addiction, and eat away at their savings to say, "Hmm, that looks like it destroys homes and makes people poor. I think I'll avoid that."

You have a choice. You can learn from either your own pain or someone else's pain. There are countless examples of how not to do life. You don't have to experience it yourself to learn how painful something is.

> Every decision you make will have either a positive or a negative effect on your life, and there are a few decisions that are absolute deal breakers.

Wayne Cordeiro, pastor of New Hope Church in Hawaii, says that the average person makes about three hundred choices every day: when to get up, what to wear, what to eat, whom to call, what to tackle first at home, school, or work. Of those three hundred choices, about thirty of them have potentially life-altering outcomes: which relationships should I pursue, should I go to college and where, is it time to start a family, should I consider that job offer, do I try to beat this red light?[2]

To narrow it even further, Erwin McManus says that "most of us can summarize our lives around five or six defining decisions—decisions that if we'd chosen differently would have radically altered the trajectory of our lives."[3]

One decision can cause years of regret, while another can produce a lifetime of benefit. Every decision you make will have either a positive or a negative effect on your life, and there are a few decisions that are absolute deal breakers. It's your life, and you have the freedom to choose. But after fifty-three years of watching and listening to hundreds of people who have either succeeded or failed, my advice is to avoid the fatal fall.

PART 3

Breakthroughs for the Broken

10

Everybody Needs a Fred

One thing I know is that every person has a dark side. You have personality and character flaws that you might not be aware of, but they are there. I have them too, many of them. Some of us have huge cracks, gaping holes that everyone else can see but often escape our notice. Some of you wonder why you fail to sustain close friendships or an intimate marriage or consistently get passed over at work.

It could be a relating pattern that pushes people away, and you're not even aware of it. It could be that you talk too much, don't listen, roll your eyes at others' suggestions, or sigh in meetings, which communicates boredom or disgust. Maybe you're irritable, cranky, moody, easily miffed; maybe you're loud, arrogant, short-tempered, or selfish. Maybe you never pick up the tab, don't tip, and are rude to waiters and store clerks. Maybe you can't hold a confidence, which is why nobody wants to get close. Maybe you tend to power up and push your agenda. These are character flaws that negatively affect everything and everyone you touch. Deeper, darker flaws include dishonesty, anger, addictions, or sexual immorality.

A question members of our leadership team ask is, "What's it like to be on the other side of me?" That's a scary question to throw on the table, because if your colleagues are honest, they will come up with two or three flaws that get in the way of your personal and professional performance. These are character issues. And I repeat, we all have them. The question is, do you know what yours are? Because you can't manage or correct them if you don't.

It wasn't until I reached my fifties that I became somewhat self-aware and actually knew a thing or two about myself and about life in general. Seriously, what do you really know when you're in your twenties? Not much. In your thirties, you're consumed with proving your worth and climbing the ladder. In your forties, you've either found your groove or you spend all your energy trying to fix whatever you wrecked in your thirties. It's only in your fifties that you actually know anything, because you have more life behind you than you have in front of you.

By God's grace and a lot of family support, I was able to avoid any sort of fatal fall in my twenties, thirties, and forties. Even though I went through some very lean years, I never made any life-altering mistakes. I got a great education, was never fired from a job, married a wonderful Christian girl, had two great kids, and kept advancing in my career.

But something happened to me in my early forties that was very confusing to me. The church I was leading was growing by 20 percent or more each year, and a couple years it grew by 40 percent. We were building buildings and adding staff, and the number of requests for me to lead and teach outside our church were increasing. Eventually, I was asked to lead the preaching department at Bethel Theological Seminary as a permanent part-time professor; I couldn't have scripted my life any better. Everything I was doing seemed to fit who I was.

But about two years into it, I was miserable. I didn't see it at the time, but the demands on my life had outgrown my ability to keep up. I felt tethered to so many people and obligations that one day I took my canoe out to a local lake in the driving rain, paddled out to the middle, and just sat there for two hours. With rain and tears streaming down my face, I looked up toward the gray sky and said out loud, "What's wrong with me?" What confused me was that everything I was doing was good. But doing all of it was slowly sucking the life out of me.

Danger Signs

The cracks started showing up in harsh comments and bursts of anger toward my wife, kids, and staff. I had become a virtual recluse at the office. My staff no longer had access to me. I sequestered myself behind my door, because I had to crank out a sermon, lesson plan, or news article. Tensions between my staff and me were completely dismissed and swept under the rug. If someone got hurt, it was tough luck, suck it up, and just do your job. There was no relating. Just get it done, and don't bother me, because I was in demand and people should understand that.

I was even worse at home. I was a brooding and angry man who reacted to the smallest things with hurtful comments and gestures. The kids learned to stay clear and wondered quietly to my wife, "Why is Dad like that all the time?"

Between Laurie and me there was plenty of yelling and tears, followed by days of staying out of each other's way. But I was blind to my problems and didn't understand why I felt or behaved that way. I thought everybody else was the problem and that they just didn't understand my world. I excused my behavior because I truly believed I was doing what God had led me to do. And that was true, I *was* doing what God had led me to do, only I was doing too much of it.

I had a sense that something inside me was breaking, but I didn't have the time or energy to address it. I was also too afraid to allow anyone to have access to my soul.

Emotionally, I was depleted, and it showed up in my inability to love or laugh. Bill Hybels once said, "The way I was doing God's work was destroying the work of God in me."[1] My inability to love or laugh manifested itself in a very painful way on a family trip to the north shore on Lake Superior at a place called Blue Fin Bay.

After four hours on the road, we unpacked our stuff at Blue Fin, and I discovered that I had packed all the skis but no ski boots, which was just enough to tip me over the edge. I voiced my frustration by saying things like, "How can I be expected to keep track of everything? How can I be responsible for the kids' stuff, my stuff, and everybody else's stuff? No wonder I forget stuff!" I was blowing off steam that had been building for weeks. By day three my lousy mood had pretty much ruined the entire trip, but I thought maybe a three-mile family hike to Carlton Peak along the Superior National Trail would lift our spirits. When I mentioned the hike to my family, I should've picked up on the silence, but I guilted them into going—in the fog, in silence, in protest.

Finally, about halfway up the mountain I stopped, turned around, and began lecturing everyone about their attitude, about family vacations. I said, "Is this the thanks I get for trying to plan a fun outing?" Two of four family members started crying, and the other two were just plain mad, so we turned around—in the fog, in silence, in protest.

That afternoon it was quiet around the condo. I'd gone off to my room by myself; the others had gone off by themselves. But an hour later I heard a soft knock on my door, and it was my fourteen-year-old daughter, Meggie. She walked into my room and handed me a card that she'd made. Then without saying anything, she turned and walked away.

With different colored markers she had written on the outside:

DAD.

On the inside it said,

I'M SORRY FOR HAVING A BAD ATTITUDE, FOR RUINING YOUR TIME AND FOR BEING SELFISH PLEASE FORGIVE ME. LOVE, MEGAN

She had drawn four little hearts near her name, and it broke *my* heart, because I was the one who had the bad attitude. I was the one who was angry. I was the one God had to change, not my daughter, son, or wife. Meg doesn't know this, but I hung on to her note for a full year, and every time I read my Bible and wrote in my journal, I looked at Meg's note and was reminded over and over again, every day, for a full year that the person who needed to change the most in my family was *me*. But I didn't know how.

■The Moment of Truth

So God in his wisdom and grace sent me a messenger. Just like God sent the prophet Nathan to confront King David with his sin, God sent Dean Hager to confront me. Dean respected my teaching and leadership, and so one day he wrote me a personal letter saying how God had been nudging him to find a role to play at Eagle Brook. One thing led to another, and after a couple years of being in a mentoring group together, Dean became our church chairman.

One of the reasons Dean agreed to the role was because he wanted to help me become a better leader. As he got closer to me, he saw some of the deeper cracks, so he decided that the best way he could help me was to empower the board to help me work on my leadership skills. But when Dean dug further into it, he began hearing disturbing rumblings from staff and lay leaders about my relating patterns. Dean has always had a unique ability to discern a train wreck in the making, and this train was headed toward a big crash.

Dean spent several months interviewing key lay leaders and staff. He always kept me abreast of what was being said and what he thought I (and the board) should do. I knew there were some serious problems, but I didn't know how serious until a board meeting in February 2004.

Dean had gained the full trust of the board *and* me, and he knew it was time to call for an executive meeting with my leadership role as the only agenda. Dean summarized his concerns, and though I had spent fourteen years leading our church, Dean said to the board, "The question before us tonight is this: is Bob Merritt the one who should continue to lead us?"

I was so stunned that I couldn't speak. To have that question raised shook me to the core. I realized that these eight people held my fate in their hands, and at that moment I knew I had some serious flaws to overcome or I'd lose almost everything I'd given my life to.

■Fred

The consensus that night was that I was still the guy they wanted to lead our church, but it came with a condition: I would enter a yearlong intervention with a leadership coach whose name was Fred. Fred has an office in Minneapolis, and he coaches CEOs throughout the country. The year would be filled with numerous one-on-one interviews with Fred, taking every personality profile under the sun, and with Fred facilitating several group interventions between the board and me.

Fred and his assistant interviewed all my family members, most of my staff, and all of my closest friends using sixty questions that essentially asked, "What's good about Bob, and what's bad about Bob?" Those interviewed held nothing back, and their candid responses were recorded in a two-hundred-page document that Fred and his assistant read back to me, word for word, during a two-day meeting. When my leadership team asked me what that was like, the phrase "it felt like a leadership vasectomy" came out of my mouth. I felt completely exposed. And snipped.

For two solid days I sat in a chair and listened to Fred read statements like, "Bob overlooks relationships and lacks interpersonal skills in working with people." "Bob doesn't listen well." "Bob doesn't manage his staff." "There's no love." "He's unapproachable." "Bob speaks before he thinks." "Bob has a love problem." "I know that Bob cares, but he's not gifted in showing it."

For two days I listened to page after page of how people didn't think I cared about them and how I'd been dismissive and hurtful toward them. I heard repeatedly that I needed to manage my mouth and measure my words and body language carefully. My colleagues and friends said some affirming things about my teaching and leadership, but what I learned is that those things get lost and don't matter if I'm a jerk.

But what really nailed me was when I heard these words from my son, David: "My dad is angry a lot." When Fred read those words to me, he looked up from the page and let them sink into my soul. I had to look away. After several seconds of silence, Fred offered some loving words of counsel and solace, but I was unable to hear him. I couldn't get past the raw emotion that I was feeling. I couldn't believe I had been so blind, that instead of love, laughter, and kindness, my son was experiencing anger from me. It wrecked me. Never in my life had I been so convicted of how flawed I was.

■Broken

When you hear the same themes repeated over and over again from a variety of people who've experienced what it's like to be on the other side of you, you know the truth. You can hear the same themes from your kids or your spouse, but you tend to blow them off. You assume they're just ticked off about something or they're being hypercritical. You hear them, but you dismiss them. But when person after person says, "Bob doesn't listen well," or "Bob uses hurtful words a lot," or "I don't feel like I could ever approach Bob with honest feedback," you know that you might have some issues. It became clear to me that it wasn't very pleasant to be on the other side of Bob Merritt. Fred put the mirror up to my face, and for the first time I saw the ugly cracks.

It broke me.

I was embarrassed and deeply saddened.

And it was the beginning of my new life.

Part of what confused me was that I had been successful doing what I had always done and behaving the way I'd always behaved. Why was I running into so many problems now?

I learned a vital leadership lesson: what got you where you are won't get you where you need to go. Instead of leading a church of three hundred, I was now leading a church of ten thousand. Instead of leading three staff members, I was now leading two hundred. What worked before wouldn't work anymore; the landscape had changed. And when the landscape changes, you have to change with it. The number of people and systems depending on my leadership had multiplied exponentially, which meant that my leadership abilities had to grow in order for the church and my life to go forward.

Talent Isn't Enough

I had always thought that as long as I delivered the goods, that was good enough. As long as I taught well, led well, and didn't screw up, that's all that was required. But I learned that being a competent teacher and leader wasn't enough. People expected me to be nice. Imagine that! They wanted me to be conversant, approachable, and interested in their lives. They wanted to have some access to my time and actually have some sort of relationship with me.

I began seeing for the first time that talent can take you only so far. I was getting As on the talent side but Fs on the relationship side. And what Fred and others were saying to me was that if I didn't start getting some Cs and Bs on the relationship side, I could take my talent and go find another job. I was on the verge of losing my staff, because instead of feeling encouraged and empowered by me, they felt devalued and defeated. What's worse is that my staff had begun to adopt some of my bad habits, because the leader sets the tone and pace.

I've never had much trouble doing the task side of my job; it's been the relationships side where I've had a consistent struggle. If I could improve that side of the equation, the possibilities for influence and achievement would multiply, because then we'd be doing things as a team. And a good team always outperforms individual talent—always.

I think part of the reason I failed to see the value in teaming up with other people was that for so many years I had led solo, and it seemed like everything depended on me. I had to pay my way through school, get my papers written, recruit volunteer youth leaders, plan the youth retreat, arrange for the bus, even drive the bus. When I got my first full-time job as a pastor in Falun, Wisconsin, I had no staff, so in addition to writing messages and finding musicians, I put together the weekly bulletin, photocopied them, and ran them through the folding machine. I did everything but hand them out on Sunday morning. For the first twenty years of my professional life, I was a one-man wrecking crew. I had some volunteer help, but I carried the mother lode, and it seemed like people were happy to let me carry it.

But then things started to grow and become complex. There were more programs, processes, and meetings; more worship services, Bible studies, and small group functions. In short, there were more people, and I had never learned how to lead people well, because I never really had to. I mostly did my own thing without people. When I *had* to enlist the help of others, I had enough relating skills to get by. If I would happen to lose my temper, power up, or cut people off, most of them let it go and attributed it to my youthful immaturity. Almost nobody had the courage or permission to confront me with the ugly truth. And that's what landed me in front of Fred.

■Was Change Possible?

The question that haunted me was, *could* I change? Marcus Buckingham asks, "How much of a person can you change?" His response is, "Not much."[2] You are who you are. And that's true. You are who God made you to be, created uniquely in his image. Much of who we are is hardwired into us.

But all of us pick up some additional junk along the way. We pick up weird ways of relating from our parents, siblings, friends, and TV that become habitual and hurtful. The goal was to identify the flaws that were a product of my own sin and selfishness and deal with them. The goal was to become aware of and correct my destructive patterns around the office and at home.

For example, Fred's data revealed that my body language and facial expressions were often dismissive and belittling to people, and so I lost credibility with board members, architects, consultants, and other leaders without even knowing it. I learned that my mood swings were potent and that my choice of words carried enormous weight. I unknowingly violated basic leadership rules like "Praise in public, admonish in private." I had a habit of admonishing in public and not giving much praise at all. This diminished my leadership and staff morale.

These are the things that Dean and Fred began to teach me and to which they held me accountable. I still slip up, especially when I'm depleted, and I have ongoing tune-ups with Fred, because lifelong patterns are difficult to overcome. But letting a professional counselor probe around in my life saved my career, renewed my marriage, blessed my kids, and caused our church to surge to new heights. I always thought I could avoid the proverbial crack-up. I'd read about other leaders who'd blown it and thought it would never happen to me. I was smarter than that. But there I was.

Permission to Breathe

One of the things Fred said I had to do immediately was resign my teaching role at Bethel Seminary. When he evaluated my life, he wondered why I hadn't collapsed already. He told me that no human being could sustain the pace I was keeping without doing severe damage to their soul and relationships. He said it was a deal breaker.

Who's your Fred?

Why did I need to have a professional tell me that? Part of it was that I was filling a genuine need that Bethel had in the preaching department, and it seemed to be working. I was able to add value to young preachers, and what could be more honorable than that? Again, how could something so good be so wrong? The other part is that you don't know where the wall is until you hit it. Burnout was new territory for me. So I kept adding more roles and responsibilities, because I didn't know my limits. Eventually, however, I found myself in a position where the demands exceeded my ability to meet them. But I didn't know how to get out of it. I felt like I would be letting people down if I stepped away from my obligations.

Fred gave me the permission I needed to resign, and that single decision probably saved my career and kept me out of the loony bin. After three years of being away from Bethel, I agreed to go back and teach a one-week intensive preaching class. I was breathing again.

Who's your Fred? Who has access to your life and has permission to give you honest feedback about your flaws? Who has permission to take the scalpel and skillfully cut out the character cancers that maybe you can't see but if not dealt with will eat away at your life? Proverbs 12:15 says, "The way of a fool seems right to him, but a wise person listens to advice." For about forty-eight years, I thought my way of leading and behaving was the right way, and I had a decent track record to back it up. But the Bible says that only fools think that way. Only fools think that their way is the only right way. On the other hand, it says that a wise person listens to advice. Wise people admit they don't have all the answers; instead, they seek out advice from others who are wiser and further down the road than they are.

> Wise people admit they don't have all the answers; instead, they seek out advice from others who are wiser and further down the road than they are.

Do you remember football coach Mike Holmgren? I was sitting in O'Hare Airport on Christmas Day in 1996. I picked up the *Chicago Tribune* and saw an article I have saved for nine years. Holmgren is considered the best quarterback coach in the history of the game; he's coached Joe Montana, Steve Young, Brett Favre, and others. In the article, Holmgren said, "I watch every snap my quarterbacks take. I've watched thousands of snaps in practice, and you see little things, little tendencies and flaws that could make all the difference in a win or loss."[3]

He watches every snap the quarterback takes; not every pass, play, or handoff; every *snap*. Here's my question: who's watching your snaps? Who's watching every snap you take to help make you better. Everyone has at least one flaw or habit that tends to hurt relationships and performance. If someone were to watch your snaps, they could help you become a better person.

Three Vital Questions

Why Aren't More People Open to Receiving Help or Advice?

Some people think that if they ask for help it's a sign of weakness. But the reverse is actually true: asking for help is a sign of strength and courage. Everyone around you already knows your flaws, so when you admit you need some help, it shows that you're becoming more self-aware. When the board saw that I was genuinely open to receiving help, they rallied around me. They viewed it as a strength, not a weakness.

Another reason why people don't seek advice is because doing so requires change, and change is uncomfortable and requires work. It's not easy to put a magnifying glass to your flaws; it can be embarrassing. And it means you have to put effort into changing. Some people simply don't want to do the hard work.

Another reason people close themselves off from advice is because they're afraid they won't be *able* to change. It might mean more failure, and they're not sure they can handle that. So they make excuses for their behavior and say things like, "That's just who I am." But excuses keep people stuck and confined to a life of low achievement.

What Compels People to Seek Advice?

I think the two driving forces behind those who seek help are fear and pain.

Fear is a powerful emotion. I was genuinely afraid of losing my job. I was frightened into getting help. Once I started getting answers to my problems and what I had to do to fix them, the fear subsided.

Fear comes from the unknown. If I'm in the dark about how I'm performing or how I'm being perceived, that causes me to be afraid. But if everything's on the table, then I know what I'm dealing with. Nothing frightens me more than when a board member or leadership team member says to me, "I'm concerned about something. Can I talk to you about it *tomorrow*?" That kills me, because my mind wanders all over the place wondering what I did wrong. Tell me now or just shoot me. The unknown scares me. Getting the issue out on the table, even if it's ugly, reduces the fear because at least now I know.

The other motivator for seeking advice is pain. Pain is a powerful incentive. Unfortunately, some people wait until the pain is so severe that it's too late. They have a heart attack, and then they get advice on diet and exercise. They lose their marriage, and then they join a support group. They become depleted to the point of losing their job, and then they solicit the help of a life coach. They watch their teenager run away from home, and then they get motivated to attend church as a family.

Pay attention to the pain levels in your life. Pain is God's way of telling us that something's out of whack and needs attention. Fear and pain are signals that you might need outside help.

What's the Difference between Those Who Get Better and Those Who Don't?

When I started seeing Fred, I told him I was afraid that I might not be able to change. Fred has seen hundreds of CEO types, and he says that the success rate is around 40 percent. The other 60 percent continue to stumble and often end up losing their jobs and families. He said that the difference is humility. Those who turn the corner and take their leadership and lives to a new level are those who are humble enough to receive the feedback and take it seriously. They demonstrate a sincere willingness to look at the data, accept it, and commit to work on it. James 4:10 says, "Humble yourselves before the Lord, and he will lift you up." That verse is absolutely true. It's not the prideful and arrogant whom God raises up; it's the humble. Humble yourself before God, and he will raise you up. In other words, the way up is down.

So if you've hit a wall, are worn out, or are confused; if you're afraid and somewhat paranoid about what others are saying about you, thinking about you, even conspiring against you; if you're angry, alone, and feeling misunderstood, I urge you to ask these three questions: First, am I genuinely open to receiving feedback? Second, am I experiencing fear and pain in my relationships? And third, will I be humble enough to address the cracks?

■A Second Chance

A year after Fred started digging around in my life, my family went up to the north shore again, and it was day three. It was a crystal clear morning with a blue sky. A foot of fresh snow had quietly fallen overnight, and it was seven degrees. It'd been a great three days; I had made sure of it. And we were just hanging out by the fire when Meg came up to me and said, "Hey, Dad, wanna take a hike to Carlton Peak?"

My wife looked up from her novel and smiled. This was a gift from God, and I knew it. This was Meg's way of forgiving me for what had happened the year before. For a full year I'd carried that failure in my heart, and I knew God was giving me a second chance. It was just me and Meg, dad and daughter.

It was a postcard morning. The sun sparkled off the fresh snow, and when we stepped out of the truck, our boots disappeared in white powder. We cut our own path up through the spruce trees, whose branches sagged with new snow. We inched our way around the steep boulders near the summit, and we reached Carlton Peak about an hour later with rosy cheeks and coats unzipped. We looked out over miles of pure white that cascaded into the deep blue expanse of Lake Superior.

There are certain moments in life that God gives you that can't be captured in print. This was one of them. Meg and I stood on that peak, and neither of us could say a word. I reached over and hugged her with both arms, and she returned the hug. That was our moment, a God moment that can never be repeated. And we drank it in with pure joy and gratitude. Every time I think about that day my eyes get moist and I get a lump in my throat.

Then we dared each other to slide down one-hundred-foot drop-offs. We held hands and slid on our butts, spraying snow and laughing like a couple of third-graders. I should be dead. Thanks to God and Fred, I'm more alive today than I think I've ever been.

In Psalm 139, King David prayed, "Search me, O God, and . . . see if there is any offensive way in me" (vv. 23–24). That's hard to do, to slice open your soul to God and ask him to search all through your being. What would God find in you that is offensive and flawed? It can be painful. But that's where breakthroughs begin, because the way up is down. Humble yourself before God, and he will lift you up.

Everybody needs a Fred.

11

Hope at the Duck's Breath Saloon

Sometimes change seems impossible. Stories abound about people who've tried all kinds of formulas, therapy, techniques, self-help books, and gimmicks to try to change something that's harmful in their life. And while these things might help for a while, most of these people fall back into their same old habits and patterns, and they just give up. Maybe that's your story. It's certainly been mine. I become aware of a flaw or destructive pattern, I ask God to help me overcome it, I gain control over it for a season, but then I slip back into old ways. In his book *I Really Want to Change . . . so Help Me God*, James MacDonald writes:

> The number one reason we don't change is because at some time in the past we have attempted to change, and then failed, and in the process we get hurt and defeated. After trying a few times, we just give up. We conclude that the only pain worse than needing to change is trying to change and failing.[1]

Larry Crabb, author and expert on spiritual change, once said, "I've been a follower of Jesus for over fifty years now, and I am appalled, after all these years, at how untransformed I really am."[2]

But the Bible promises that God can change a human life, and while change *seems* impossible, it's not. It's hard, it's a lifelong process, it's sometimes frustrating and painful, but it's not impossible.

Three years ago I met a man named Jim Grannen who thought change was impossible. Jim and his wife, Jeanie, were staying at the Black Forest Inn just a few doors down from Laurie and me in the Black Hills of South Dakota. When I first saw Jim, he had dismounted his Harley and was strolling toward the deck where I was reading *Created to Be God's Friend* by Henry Blackaby. Jim sported a red bandana, blue jeans, ponytail, and a long, gray beard. He slowly made his way up the steps of the deck, sat down, and leaned back in a patio chair next to me. He lifted his black leather boots onto the wooden footrest, lit a cigarette, nodded my way, and said, "How ya doin'?" I covered the title to my book and thought, "If this guy finds out I'm a pastor, he'll flip."

I nodded his way and said, "Not bad. How you doin'?" No response.

I said, "You a part of the rally?" (Every year sixty thousand Harley bikers descend on Sturgis, South Dakota, in the Black Hills for the annual rally.)

He said in a thick southern drawl, "Yeah. Me and the wife come out every year."

I said, "Really. What's the attraction?"

He said, "Oh, you know—ride around, look at the chrome."

I thought, "That's worth a trip to South Dakota every year?" But I said, "Sounds fun."

He said, "You ride?"

"I used to ride a Suzuki 185." He looked at me, smiled, then took a long drag on his cigarette as he looked out over the hills.

But I sensed there was something going on inside Jim, so the next morning I sat at his breakfast table and asked him if he'd tell me his story. He said, "Do you have an hour?" I said, "I'm in South Dakota." I pulled out my notepad and wrote down what Jim said:

I'm fifty-two years old, but September 9, 1980, was the day the best part of my life began. I came out of Vietnam a hard drinker and drug addict, and it was killin' me, killin' my wife, and killin' my two kids. And I knew it, but alcohol had a hold on me. I'd be drivin' home from work, it was a twenty-five-mile drive, and I had to fight the urge to stop at the bars. Night after night I'd fight it all the way to the last bar, but then I'd pull in and order a drink with tears in my eyes.

Sometimes you wake up in life and you don't know where you are, where you've been, or where you're going. I pulled over in the driving rain one night in my beat-up '74 Buick Skylark, and I had no idea where I was or where I was going. I lived in Atlanta, but I wound up in a jail in Macon, Georgia, with a DWI, and I didn't know how I got there.

In the meantime, Jeanie had joined Al-Anon and was gettin' on with her life; she was gettin' healthy and that scared me to death. I was losing my wife—she'd kicked me out of the house. I was losing my life, I was running out of sick leave from work, but I couldn't stop myself.

I was on a binge that was impossible for me to shake, which brings me to September 9, 1980. That night I went to the Duck's Breath Saloon, where I had my final drink, because the next day I checked myself into the hospital.

And then Jim said words that blew me away. He said, "The next day, I stepped onto the rubber pad that opens the automatic doors to the hospital, and that was the moment. I didn't say 'God' or 'Jesus,' but that was the moment I gave my life to him. But after ten days of treatment, the hospital staff said I'd never make it and that I was a hopeless case."

Jim leaned across the table, looked me in the eye, and said, "Rehab and AA can help you get free from alcohol, but what really did it for me was Jesus. Without him, you can become free of alcohol, but you'll never have the joy and freedom that only Jesus brings."

Today Jim's been free from alcohol for twenty-five years. He works for Medical Doctor Associates as director of government contracting and generates fifteen million dollars of business for his company annually. Jim is a changed man.

■We Can Change

Maybe it's not an addiction to alcohol that's got a hold on you, but maybe it's depression, or guilt, or some secret habit. Maybe you feel numb, or passionless, or plain ol' blah. Maybe you're just drifting without any purpose or direction. Maybe you've never felt close to God. Maybe like Jim Grannen you woke up one day and didn't know where you were or how you got there, and you feel lost and alone. The great news is that if God can change a guy who staggered into a hospital and was told he'd never make it, God can change you. He can change me. There's hope at the Duck's Breath Saloon, and with God's help you and I can change whatever's broken inside of us and start a new life.

James 3:2 says, "We all stumble in many ways." That could be my life verse. I'm pretty sure I do or say something wrong every day. Some days I'm embarrassingly sinful. The reality is that even if we've begun a new life in Christ, we will still sin. We will still be angry, afraid, and selfish; we will still say things and do things that hurt people. Even if we're forgiven, there's still this gap between who we are and who we want to become. The good news is that's completely normal. The bad news is that closing the gap between the real and the ideal is a lifelong pursuit of growth that requires humility and discipline.

But with God's help, you and I can change whatever is sinful, harmful, or broken in our lives. The Bible tells us repeatedly that we can change. Jim's story shows us that nobody's a hopeless case, the power of Christ to change people is real, and forgiveness and grace are available to any who ask for it. Forgiveness doesn't free us from some of the long-term scars and consequences that come from a careless past. But it gives us a new start with the possibility for a better future. It's never too late to rebuild your life. The question is, how does change happen?

Look at what the Bible says about life change:

> Do not copy the behavior and customs of this world, but let God transform you into a new person by changing the way you think. (Rom. 12:2 NLT)

> Those who become Christ-followers become new people. They are not the same anymore. The old life is gone, a new life has come. (2 Cor. 5:17, author paraphrase)

> He who began a good work in you will carry it on to completion until the day of Christ Jesus. (Phil. 1:6)

The Bible tells us that God wants to *transform*, *renew*, and *complete* us, which means that transformation and change are fundamental themes in the Bible. The Bible wouldn't instruct us to change if change weren't possible. The goal isn't *just* salvation but transformation. The goal isn't *just* to get to heaven someday; the goal is to shed the old life and start living a new one long before heaven. Romans 12:2 says, "Let God transform you into a new person."

How Do We Change?

Whenever I talk about change, some people get nervous because they think they have to change their personality, or become a religious fanatic, or become someone they're not. I once interviewed actor Stephen Baldwin on our stage, and when I asked him about doing movies and playing some roles that were somewhat sketchy, I'll never forget what he said: "God doesn't want me to stop being Stephen Baldwin. He just wants me to stop sinning."

I love that! Being transformed doesn't mean you lose your personality or passions; it doesn't mean you become all religious, weird, or soft. I'm still nuts about hunting, golf, biking, canoeing, and fishing. I love watching sports and listening to country music. God doesn't want me to stop being Bob Merritt. He just wants me to stop sinning.

> The goal is to shed the old life and start living a new one long before heaven.

But how?

Change is rarely immediate; instead, it's a process. And it never really ends. There are starts and stops, progress and regress, but over time, as you practice better relating patterns and habits, you'll notice that you fail less and rebound quicker. The following four steps are crucial for lasting change to happen.

Let God

The Bible says, "Let *God* transform you." It doesn't say, "Let Dr. Phil's booty camp change you," or "Let Tony Robbins's power of positive thinking change you," or "Let Oprah's 'spirit' change you." There's not a single person, program, book, or technique that can change your life. Your spouse can't change you; neither can your boss, mom, or therapist. You can't even change yourself. Only *God* can change a human life. Which means that practicing new habits or incorporating new disciplines can take you only so far. Ultimately, God is the only one who can change a human being and put that person on a new path.

Yet how many people run from fad to fad, to therapy, seminars, psychics, yoga, or motivational speakers, often paying huge sums of money to try to bring about the change that only God can produce? In our newspaper business section awhile back, I read, "The Psychic Friends Network filed for bankruptcy." Their lawyer said, "Apparently they made some bad decisions due to *unforeseen* circumstances." Hello! Only God can change us into new people. But how often do we turn to God as a last resort? When all else has failed, maybe we give God a try.

Two weeks before Christmas our bathtub was clogged. In the past, I'd been able to fish out the slop with a makeshift hook and wire, but this time I'd only made it worse. I had pushed everything down the drain farther and farther. After battling for an hour, I finally went to the hardware store to get a snake, because there's no way Liquid Drano would work—that's all advertising hype. So I bought a middle-of-the-road-quality snake for fifteen dollars, sped back home, and ran the snake down the hole. Turns out the snake was the wrong style, but the label says you can't exchange it because of sanitary reasons. I was sitting there in the tub, and I almost said a bad word, but it was close to Christmas, so I controlled myself, I think.

I drove back to the hardware store, bought a new and improved snake, but I could not unclog the drain. Finally, after several hours of frustration and losing my cool, after thirty-five dollars down the same drain, Laurie said, "Maybe Liquid Drano would work."

I said, "No way. But if you want to pick some up the next time you're out, go ahead. What can it hurt?"

> Only God can change a human life.

That stuff is like the Holy Spirit of God. It goes down the drain, sees where the grime is, and goes right to work. Without any effort on my part, Liquid Drano does what I'm incapable of doing: it clears the pipes and cleans up the mess. And this is so typical. I try to change whatever's wrong in my life, and only after I've messed it all up do I realize, "There's nothing I can do about this. I need to rely on the miracle-working power of Liquid Drano; I need a power that's beyond me." (I've since learned that a plunger does the job better than anything.)

And notice that we have to *let* God do it. The Bible says, "*Let* God transform you into a new person." God doesn't force us to change; we have to let him, which means we have to surrender our control to him.

Jim Grannen said, "I didn't say 'God' or 'Jesus,' but that was the moment I gave my life to him." Jim came to a place where he knew he needed Jesus—not church, not another person or program, but Jesus. Unless you can point to a moment or time when you turned to Jesus and asked him to enter your life, it'll be impossible for you to change. Paul described it this way in Galatians 2:20: "I now live my earthly life by trusting in Jesus" (author paraphrase).

Some of you may need to do that for the very first time. Jesus told us in Revelation 3:20 that he stands at the door of our heart knocking, and if we let him in, he will come in and start a new relationship that brings forgiveness, healing, and joy. Jesus never forces his way into someone's life; he stands outside knocking. You may have sensed him knocking from time to time, but maybe you've never invited Jesus to save you. Maybe you've never put your trust in him.

Jesus said, "I have come that you may have life, and have it to the full" (John 10:10). If you sense that something is missing, if you keep making the same mistakes over and over again and nothing ever changes, the first step is to invite Jesus Christ into your life so that he can forgive you and start cleaning out whatever has you stuck.

And that can be scary, because when you begin to let God change you, he will show you things in your life that are clogging the drain. I don't know if you've ever seen the black, smelly sludge that clogs drains, but it's nasty. It's painful to look at. But until that sin is forgiven and cleaned out, you will be stuck in the same old patterns. And some of that stuff's been down there for years—anger, resentment, greed, lust, sexual misconduct, self-pity, deception, envy, pettiness, arrogance. But change can't happen until we invite God into our lives and let him clean out the darkness.

Why should you do it? Why should you open yourself up to letting God change you? If you don't let God change whatever's wrong and destructive in your life, you will experience ongoing decay and death. Galatians 6:7–8 says, "Don't be misled. Remember, you can't ignore God and get away with it. Those who live according to their own sinful desires will harvest the consequences of decay and death" (author paraphrase). Letting God clean out the sin in my life is scary, but what's scarier is living with the same old habits and patterns that could wreck my marriage, destroy my kids, harm my friendships, tank my career, and waste my potential, causing me to miss out on the life God has planned for me.

So if you're not seeing anything change in your life, the question has to be asked: have you ever invited Jesus in to forgive, cleanse, and change you? Because it's impossible to change without God in your life. "*Let* God change you into a new person."

Identify Your Specific Sins

For change to happen, we have be honest about and identify specific sins that hinder progress. James MacDonald writes, "If you're serious about transformation you must be willing to ask God what specific thing he wants to change in you. Until you get specific, transformation will be a pipedream."[3] So here's my question: can you name the specific sin, habit, pattern, attitude, or behavior that is damaging to you and others? What specific thing does God want to change in you? If you're having trouble thinking of it, then ask your spouse, they'll be glad to tell you. Ask your friends or co-workers; ask your kids.

Several years ago I was preparing a message for Easter, and so I was thinking about what sin I needed to give up for Lent. I thought, "Why not ask my kids?" I have found this to be a good but sobering practice. You might get some feedback that's difficult to hear, but it could save you some grief down the road.

We were sitting around the table, so I looked over at Dave, who was slurping down some potato soup—he was ten at the time. I said, "So, Dave, what sin do I have in my life that I need to get rid of?"

He looked up at me, wiped his mouth on his sleeve, and said, "Sin, Dad? Isn't it more like sins?"

I said, "Whatever."

He said, "Your temper." (This was before Fred.)

I said, "Really?"

He said, "Yeah, sometimes you lose it, like the time you grabbed my shirt and yelled at me. And how about the time you . . ."

I said, "Okay, okay, I'll try to work on that."

Meg was sitting over there chomping at the bit. "Bad words," she said.

I said, "What do you mean bad words?"

"Like the time we were in the car and you were in a hurry; you said a bad word, Dad."

I said, "You're right—occasionally I let one slip. I'll try to work on that."

I thought they were done, but they were just warming up. Finally, I couldn't take it anymore, so I turned the discussion away from me and said, "What about your mother?" which wasn't smart.

Laurie said, "Don't drag me into this; you have enough sins to keep us talking all afternoon."

The point is that you and I can't work on changing something we can't see or don't think is a problem. How can you overcome anger if you don't see that it's a problem, or alcoholism, or materialism, or lust, or bitterness, or a critical spirit? The second step to changing is to identify the specific sins God wants to rid us of and admit that they're a problem.

Starve Your Old Life and Feed Your New Life

Once you've identified the specific sins you want to over-come, the third step is to starve your old life and feed your new one. In other words, you need to start making wiser choices about the people, places, and circumstances that draw you into your areas of weakness.

The Bible tells us that when we invite Jesus into our lives, the Holy Spirit of God takes up residence inside us and never leaves us. We still have what the Bible calls a "sinful human nature" that continues to pull us toward destructive desires and behaviors, but the Holy Spirit gives us a new power to overcome those things. Essentially, we have two natures living inside us, the old sinful nature and the new spiritual nature. Which is why the Bible instructs us to "walk in the Spirit," "be led by the Spirit," and "submit to the Spirit's control." We have to make a daily choice either to allow our sinful nature to control us or to let God's Spirit control us. Romans 8:9 says, "You, however, are controlled not by the sinful nature but by the Spirit, if the Spirit of God lives in you." It's a matter of what we allow to take control of our lives. We need to starve the old life and feed the new.

Dr. Stewart Briscoe used to tell a story about the English bird called the cuckoo. It's a very large bird, but it never lays its eggs in its own nest because it never builds its own nest. It finds a nest with other eggs in it, waits until mother thrush goes away, lands, and lays its own eggs. Now you have two natures in one nest—cuckoo nature and thrush nature. Mrs. Thrush comes back, all the eggs hatch, she thinks things are a bit strange, but she goes ahead anyway. She comes back with a fat worm. One cavernous cuckoo mouth opens to greet her, and four petite thrush mouths open; two natures in one nest. One nature gets fed because the big cuckoo mouth gobbles up all the worms, and the little thrush mouths get nothing. As time goes by, the baby cuckoo grows and grows until he kicks out the baby thrushes. The nature you feed grows; the nature you starve dies.

In Romans, Paul says that if you go on pursuing the old life, feeding the old life, and hanging around the old life, it's obvious what's going to happen. The old life will continue to grow, and you will be controlled by and motivated by your sinful human nature. You'll starve God out, and you'll be forever hounded by your old habits, patterns, and sin. And change will elude you. For change to happen, you have to starve the old life and feed the new.

Once you invite Jesus into your life, that's just the beginning. Now you need to feed your new life by praying daily, reading inspirational Christian books, spending time with spiritually mature people who will help you grow, and finding a healthy place of worship. Nobody can do those things for you. You are responsible for your own spiritual growth and strength. There are a lot of defeated people whose lives haven't changed much because instead of feeding their new life with daily spiritual nutrition, they're starving it out with neglect and atrophy. Starve the old life and start feeding the new.

Begin a Lifelong Pursuit of God

Change is not an immediate event; it's a lifelong process. And the goal is not perfection but progress. Perfection is impossible, so we should stop expecting it. What we hope for is progress. As I've studied the area of transformation, I've learned that while God is capable of bringing about instantaneous, miraculous transformation, usually it's not an immediate event where you become a brand-new person who no longer struggles with temptation and sin.

Philippians 2:12 says to "work out your salvation with fear and trembling." In other words, there's a difference between salvation and transformation. Salvation happens the moment you put your trust in Jesus and ask him to come into your life; transformation is a lifelong process of becoming more like Jesus in how you live and love. Many people mistakenly think that once they put their trust in Jesus and become saved from their sins, all their problems will go away and they'll no longer be bothered by sin. Not true. Salvation is simply the beginning of the lifelong process of growth.

The Bible says work *out* your salvation, not work *for* your salvation. Now that you're saved, work it out. Work out your weaknesses, work out your behavior, work out your attitudes, work out your temptation areas. Inviting Jesus into your life saves you from sin, but it doesn't *cure* you from sinning. Now that you're saved, work it out. You didn't become an addict overnight; you worked long and hard at it. It's going to take some time, maybe the rest of your life, to work it out. You didn't develop an angry spirit overnight; some of you watched your dad or mom model that for years. It's going to take some time to work that out of your life. It took years to develop a sharp tongue, but now that you're saved, work it out; bite your tongue and clean up your language. Instead of saying, "What's wrong with you, you idiot?" practice new phrases like, "Maybe I misunderstood you" or "I wonder if we could talk about this." I have to work every day on my choice of words and tone of voice. Old habits die hard, but with God's help, they can die and you can change.

One of the ways to work out your salvation is to commit to a lifelong pursuit of God. The psalmist David said, "I run in the path of your commands, for you have set my heart free" (Ps. 119:32). His heart is set free by pursuing God and running toward his commands. This is a key element to lasting change. When you are running in pursuit of God, you tend to run away from your old, sinful ways. Galatians 5:16 says, "I advise you to live according to your new life in the Holy Spirit. Then you won't be doing what your sinful nature craves" (NLT). If you're pursuing God by making time for regular worship, incorporating a regular time of reading and praying, spending more time with good people, and finding ways to serve God with your talents and resources, you won't have the time *or* the desire to keep pursuing the old life. Paul says, "You won't be doing what the sinful nature craves." In fact, he concludes,

"The Spirit gives us desires that are the opposite of what the sinful nature desires" (Gal. 5:17 NLT). New desires like love, joy, peace, goodness, kindness, faithfulness, purity, and self-control—all of the elements that make for a better life.

What are you pursuing these days? What consumes the lion's share of your thinking and doing? Appetites are developed for things you pursue, and the moment you commit to a lifelong and daily pursuit of God, you'll begin to see changes for the good.

■The Sign of Change

How can you tell if true change has begun? Look at your relationships, because spiritual progress is always measured by the condition of our relationships. Are you quick to admit when you're wrong? Are you willing to forgive? Are you tender and kind? Do you smile at people? Do you enjoy people? Do you ever get notes from people thanking you for your kindness, generosity, or time? How are your relationships?

I've always taught that love is not a feeling; it's an action. Loving people means that I behave in loving ways toward them by forgiving them, being patient and kind toward them, overlooking faults in them, and being generous toward them. I have never *felt* like forgiving someone. Forgiveness is an act of love, a choice of the will. So I have often said, even from the platform, that the Bible commands us to *love* one another, but it never commands us to *like* one another. Thank God for that! Thank God I don't have to like everybody, because that would be impossible. Love is an action; like is a feeling. So I can forgive you (love), but I don't have to like you; I can be patient with you (love), but I don't have to like you.

But then I came across a verse in Romans 12 that says, "Don't just pretend to love others, really love them. Love each other with *genuine affection*" (v. 9, author paraphrase). Now that's a problem, because affection is sort of like a feeling, and feelings mess with my theology. But here's what I've been learning, and this has been a huge revelation to me: I have been withholding my feelings for people. I have been hiding behind the "I can love them, but I don't have to like them" idea. I have been excusing myself from having to *like* people, and consequently, my affections haven't had a chance to grow.

But God has convicted me on this, so have a few board members, staff members, family members, friends, Fred, and just about anyone who knows me. And they've challenged me to express my feelings and allow myself to get close to people. So I've tried to do that, and it's amazing. Every once in a while now I'll feel something, and it's like, "Ooh, I think that was a genuine affection." I'll catch myself smiling with people and looking forward to certain conversations and meetings. I'll never be a warm, fuzzy teddy bear. But I can tell you that having genuine affection for people is a good thing, it's a healing thing, and it's brought a whole new dimension to my life.

The best part of going to work these days is the people who are now becoming my best friends. I see other staff members sequester themselves in their offices like I used to do, and they're missing it; they're missing the best part of life. I can't believe I spent more than twenty years of my life missing out on the best part of life—friendship, laughter, and genuine love. Spiritual progress is not measured by how much you know or how long you can pray. Spiritual progress is always measured by the quality of your relationships. If you want to know if you are growing spiritually, look at your relationships. Are people an annoyance to you, or are you starting to love them "with genuine affection"?

■Quicker to Apologize

A few months ago, a colleague came to me behind stage where I was prepping to speak, and she said that the visual aid I had requested on stage would be impossible to do. We were under a lot of pressure, so in the heat of the moment I said, "I don't want to hear what's impossible right now. I want to hear what's possible." As soon as I said it, I knew I had crossed a relational line. She gently pushed back, but I pushed back harder. I said, "Look, telling me what's impossible does me no good; go back and try to figure out what's possible." I could see in her face that I had inflicted a small wound on her heart.

Fortunately, God's Holy Spirit, who lives within me, made me miserable and convicted me of my sin and wouldn't let me dismiss it. That's one of the signs of growth, by the way—when you sin and it nags at you. So twenty minutes later I sought her out and said, "I want to apologize for my anger back there. I hate it when I do that. Will you forgive me?" You know what she did? She smiled and said, "Thanks for building a bridge," and our friendship was restored. I never would have done that ten years ago. I would've blamed her and just let the chips fall. So I'm not perfect, but there's progress. I'm closing the gap between who I am and who I want to be, and that's a good sign.

The sad truth about me is that I still sin. I still think, say, and do things that make me wonder if I'll ever become the person God created me to be. Some of you may be thinking, "Bob, I want to change, but will I ever be able to treat my children the way I want to? Will I ever be able to stop hating my co-worker, classmate, ex-spouse, father, mother, brother, or sister? Will I ever be able to stop my inner rage? Will I ever be able to control my tongue? Will I ever stop trying to compete with my friend's looks, wealth, house, kids, or cars? Will I ever feel close to God? Will I ever be able to overcome my secret sin or awful habit?" The answer is yes. With God's help, you can gain victory over whatever is out of control in your life. You'll never be perfect, and you'll often slip back into old patterns, but Jesus once said, "What is impossible for people is possible with God" (Luke 18:27 NLT).

What in your life seems impossible? Jim Grannen was an impossible case, with an impossible addiction, impossible marriage, and impossible future. He didn't say the words "God" or "Jesus," but there was a moment when Jim gave his life to him. And that was the moment his new life began.

If you've had a true conversion where you've invited Jesus into your life; and if you get serious about confessing your specific sins to God, yourself, and others; if you starve your old life and feed your new one; if you develop a lifelong pursuit of God, you're going to start to change for the good. You're going to see glimmers of hope and small steps of progress. Will you fail? Yes. But you'll begin to recognize the failure quicker and confess it sooner. And true change will always show up in your relationships.

12

A Softer Soul

Life is meant to be shared. That's why God gave us marriage, children, grandchildren, and friends. It's why the average teenager sent twenty-five thousand text messages last year and why Facebook is the number one site on the internet.

Essentially, life comes down to the people in it. Think about it: if you could eat every meal at the finest restaurants, stay in the nicest hotels, sail on the biggest yachts, and travel to the most exclusive parts of the world, but you had to do it alone, what would be the point? It would all be empty. Meaning in life comes from sharing it with the people you care about. It's why my daughter calls my wife once a day, no matter where they are in the world, just to get an update.

Many years ago I toured the Taj Mahal in Agra, India, with my brother and a group of pastors. All the while we walked around this "wonder of the world," we saw a sharply dressed, European-type man taking dozens of pictures of himself. He wore a shiny suit coat with his shirt unbuttoned halfway down his hairy chest; his gold necklace and bracelet dangled about, and he seemed very impressed with himself.

Now maybe he was on business and just took a side trip to see the Taj. But the way he was posing for himself made me think otherwise. I think he was alone. And when he looks at all the pictures he took of the Taj that day, he will be in every one of them—just him. Only him. What good is traveling to great places, owning a big home, getting a new outfit, or making a hole in one if you have nobody to share it with? True joy is a shared commodity.

When I think of someone who has shared more of her life with me than I have with her, it's my mom. My mother has always been present for me, and my joy has always been her joy. But the opposite hasn't always been true; her joy has not always been my joy. I've often taken her for granted without giving much back.

When my dad died, it triggered in me a new desire to give back to my mom some of what she had given to me all my life. So I began to visit her after work, periodically bring her flowers, and invite her to join us for hamburgers on the grill on Friday evenings—little things. But I wondered what I could do that would fill my mom's joy bucket to the brim in a way that maybe she hadn't experienced since Dad died. The idea came to me three falls ago.

For ten years, my mom and dad lived in a cabin that Dad had built on their favorite lake in northern Minnesota. It was a place filled with memories of fishing, snowmobiling, berry picking, and sitting in a little country church on warm Sunday mornings. There was nothing better than going to the cabin, waking up in the morning to the sound of gentle waves slapping up against the shore, and hearing Mom scurry around downstairs getting bacon and eggs ready. Her little kitchen table was one of the most inviting spots on earth—a complete stranger felt right at home while sitting at Mom's kitchen table. Coffee was always on, and her homemade sticky buns would've put most bakeries out of business if she had gone commercial.

But at summer's end when all the visitors left and the kids went back to school, Mom and Dad found their greatest joy in taking walks together on the logging trails that wove their way through Marvin Elg's 120-acre woods. Marvin ran an old sawmill and a gravel pit behind his house. He was a man of few words but a jack-of-all-trades—right up Dad's alley. Marvin's wife, Elaine, was the church organist, and together there was nothing they couldn't do.

I think my mom and dad enjoyed those woods more than the Elgs did, and it kind of became their own. At first Dad would bring his shotgun on their walks in case they saw a grouse or two. But as they got older, he left the shotgun home and found joy in simply walking the trails hand in hand with his mate of more than fifty years.

After Dad died, the cabin was sold, and even though it was only a two-hour drive from Mom's new townhouse in White Bear Lake, she hadn't been back. She didn't know if her heart could take it, so she stayed away and rarely talked about it—until three falls ago.

Giving Back

One day I mentioned to Mom that I was going on a hunting trip to South Dakota, and she said reflectively, "I would love to go hunting again." I didn't respond immediately, but I tucked it away and began running through my mental calendar for a possible day that I could make that happen for her. My one day off each week is precious to me, and that particular fall was extremely full with an international trip in October and a trip to Dallas in November. I had one possible window, but it would have to be a last-minute decision.

The window opened, I made the call, and I asked Mom if she'd like to go up to the cabin to hunt grouse in their old woods. I could tell by the emotion in her voice that the very thought made her happy. She said she would love to go and that it would be a gift to her, but she ruled it out immediately because she was already committed to caring for my two-year-old niece and to serving on a committee at church. I told her my sister could find another babysitter and the church committee would be fine without her. So she made the calls, and we made our plans.

The next morning Mom packed a picnic lunch, I loaded the dog and hunting gear into my truck, and we took off for the two-hour drive straight north. It was a beautiful October day—the birches and poplars matched the yellow sun, the maples were ablaze in reds and orange. Seeing any grouse would be secondary, and a mere bonus, to the real gift of walking the same trails behind the old sawmill that Dad and Mom enjoyed during their last and best years together. This was more than a hunting trip; this was a return to former days of falling leaves, fresh coffee, and gentle waves splashing up against the rocks. This was their woods, their walk, and this was Mom's day. I could have been doing a dozen other things at home, but I was glad I was where I was, and I hoped something magical would happen.

About thirty minutes into our walk, I heard the unmistakable wing beat of a flushed grouse, and then another. Quickly, I turned toward the sounds with all my senses on alert. Another one flushed, but I couldn't get a shot, then another, and this time I found a brief opening as the bird darted through the trees. The shot rang out through the hardwood forest, the dog bounded into the tag alders, and her tail went wild with fresh scent. It was a great moment, one I had lived many times before—a heart-pounding flush, the first shot, the wonderful smell of a spent shotgun shell, and the soft feathers of Minnesota's most wild game bird. And my mom loved it; she loved everything about it.

I wanted to follow the birds into a swampy thicket, so I told my mom to walk higher on the ridge and stay within eyesight. I would go through the thicket and swing around to rejoin her in ten minutes. When I caught up with her, she didn't notice me right away, and it seemed like her thoughts were elsewhere. She was walking up a favorite trail that was canopied by tall maples and oaks, a trail that she and my dad walked dozens of times. I could see she was in a different time and a different day.

I gently came up behind her, and I heard her say, "Dad and I . . . ," and that's all she could say. So I put my arm around her waist, and we walked slowly up the hill together, mother and son.

In that moment, I sensed that Mom could feel Dad's love through my love, his strength through my strength. And we walked in silence, side by side up the hill, reconnecting with precious moments of earlier days.

After an hour or so, we stopped at Dad's old deer stand, which brought a few more tears. Then we continued on and found a big log, which we sat on for lunch. I prayed a short prayer before we ate our sandwiches and drank coffee from Mom's old thermos. She tossed the dog a few choice morsels, stroked Bear's head, and praised her for being such a good hunting dog. We got three birds with three shots—a near miracle for any grouse hunter.

The next day Mom brought over a grouse and rice dish served in wine sauce, and I overheard her say to my wife, "Yesterday was like a dream to me; it was magical. I can't even believe it happened."

And this is the reason for life: to share it with the ones you love most. If one day I return to the woods behind the old sawmill without my mom, I will always have *that* day, and *that* memory, and *that* joy. On that day, my mom's joy became my joy, and it was a gift that I will treasure for the rest of my life.

Maybe it's my age, or maybe I've seen enough of life to finally realize that life comes down to relationships—and not just any relationships, but the ones that have the most potential to last long and go deep, the ones that help you build a great life. These days I'm living my life with a softer soul toward people, and it's brought a new kind of joy to me that, frankly, had eluded me for most of my life.

For a large part of my life, I unknowingly looked at people for what they could do for me, how this person could help me, benefit me, support me, help me get things done. I'd come into a meeting or arrive home after work, and I expected other people to bring energy and joy to me while I just soaked it in. I wasn't doing my part to bring energy and joy to others. I sometimes wondered why I had a lot of acquaintances and not many real friends, but I never made the connection. It took some time in front of a counselor to sort some of that out, but now I make a conscious effort to bring some life to my spouse, family, staff, and friends. I try to bring energy and interest to the conversations I have, even with strangers. I try to look up from my computer when someone comes into my office with a question and give them my full attention. This communicates that "I'm listening, you're valuable to me, I'm fully engaged." These days I'm trying to give more than I take, and it's making all the difference in my *own* joy.

■Relational Integrity

This final chapter is titled "A Softer Soul," and it's about relational integrity, which is simply treating people as fellow human beings instead of treating them just as store clerks, waitstaff, or employees. It's seeing every person as an equal, created in God's image, having infinite worth—yes, marred by sin but loved and valued by God. It's understanding that every human being is a person just like you who has a real name, real fears, real needs, and a real soul that God wants to redeem, regardless of gender, race, or social status. Relational integrity is when you embrace Jesus's words in Matthew 7:12—"Do to others what you would have them do to you"—and live them out in the workplace, classroom, neighborhood, and at home. It's that simple—to treat every person you encounter exactly the way you'd want them to treat you, with kindness, generosity, patience, and forgiveness.

Relational integrity is approaching every person you en-counter as an equal who deserves your kindness and consid-eration. And it doesn't happen automatically, at least not with me. I have to remind myself and train myself over and over to treat others the way I'd like them to treat me. It's a discipline, because I can forget about relational integrity in an instant. All it takes for my humanity to go out the window is for someone to drive 35 in a 45 zone, or for someone to hog a workout machine that I'm waiting for, or for my wife to challenge a decision I make. Someone almost nudged me out of my spot in the yogurt line the other day, and it was as if they were about to commit a crime. How dare they? My natural response to these things is not to be patient, kind, and receptive but to be rude and snippy.

Last spring Laurie and I went away for a few days. We took a long walk together, and we ended up in some neighborhoods that were off the beaten track. One of the little differences Laurie and I have is that she's a stickler for rules and regu-lations, while I'm a little loosey-goosey. I certainly abide by the rules, but I've always believed that there's some wiggle room, some gray, some flexibility built into the system. And this has caused some interesting tension.

For example, I absolutely love fresh grapefruit, and I es-pecially love *free*, fresh grapefruit. So on our walk, we found a grapefruit tree that was just loaded with beautiful yellow grapefruit. It was in somebody's backyard, but its fruit-laden branches hung well over the fence. There were even a few overly ripe grapefruit that had fallen onto the public sidewalk next to this person's property. Did you notice I said *public*? Is it really private fruit if it's hanging over a very public side-walk? And truthfully, there was so much of it that there's no way the owner could have eaten it all. I've seen people just try to give it away in self-serve boxes.

So naturally I reached up to sample one, but my arm froze in midair when I heard Laurie say with disdain in her voice, "If you grab that fruit, you'll never have sex again!" That made me flinch, even though I knew she was exaggerating. If she would've said, "Touch that grapefruit and I'll be mad for a week" or "Touch it and you'll be in the doghouse," I might've gone for it and lived with the consequences. But then she said, "What do you think God thinks of that?" I hate it when she brings God into it. What followed next was a spirited debate about values, sin, and each other's screwy upbringing, but it was playful enough that we both just started laughing. In fact, I laughed so hard I couldn't even defend myself any longer.

The point is that relational integrity gets tested every day by little conflicts and annoyances. And how one responds—with either kindness or rudeness—requires discipline. When I get annoyed, I have to remind myself to chill out, take it easy, give it up, rise above it, laugh it off, and just treat the person the way I'd like them to treat me. That's all.

Relationships for the Long Haul

So with that background in mind, here's what I'm learning about relationships that go long and deep. These are some steps that have contributed to my softer soul and given me a chance at sharing life with a few others.

Start with the People around You

Your best opportunities for long and deep friendships are not in another county, state, church, or workplace. They are with the people who intersect your life on a regular basis. These may include your classmates, neighbors, or workmates, people you see and talk to on a regular basis. It's hard to have a close relationship with someone who lives or works hundreds of miles away—not impossible but difficult. As I sat around our leadership team table one day, I thought, "Why not these people? Why not spend more time with and initiate closer friendships with these people? They're in my life at least five days a week. Why not take advantage of our close proximity and build something from that?" For you it could be a neighbor down the street who's the same age, has young kids, and would love to share some life with you. But month after month, year after year, *she* sits alone behind her four walls and *you* sit alone behind your four walls, and the possibility for a relationship is missed because you think there has to be a better opportunity in some other neighborhood. But what are the chances of striking up a relationship with someone you don't even know exists? Probably none. Your best opportunities to build deeper friendships are with the people closest to you.

If you're married, the person you need to invest in the most is your spouse, and believe me, this takes effort and forethought. If Laurie and I aren't careful, we can go through months on autopilot where even though we're in the same house, we're not sharing life with each other. She does her thing, I do mine, and soon the connection is gone. There are two things that have helped us stay connected: getting away at least once a year alone together for at least seven days and serving each other in some way.

I think married couples have to get away alone together at least once a year, and it has to be far enough away so that you can't run home to mow the grass, sift through the mail, or take care of little projects. You have to disconnect from your daily life so you can reconnect with each other. And I say at least seven days because it takes awhile to detach emotionally from the dog and the kids. It also forces you to find things to do together—you can't just wait it out until you get home, because you'll go nuts. It takes awhile to slide into a rhythm where you're relating again and where you're comfortable being alone with each other. We're out in Palm Springs for ten days as I write this. After day three it began to feel long; on day four we started to ease into a rhythm, and now the days are going way too fast.

The other thing that helps Laurie and me stay connected is serving each other. In his book *The Five Love Languages*,

Gary Chapman identifies five ways people give and receive love: through receiving gifts, acts of service, physical touch, words of affirmation, and quality time.[1] Laurie feels most loved and most connected to me when I do an act of service for her.

Laurie has always found tremendous joy in having a nice-looking yard, so for fifteen years she dragged the water hoses all over our one-acre yard to keep it green. She mentioned numerous times how much she'd love a sprinkler system, but I thought it was too expensive and frivolous. Finally, an "experienced" friend of mine offered to help me put one in on the cheap, and when I told Laurie about it, she couldn't remove the smile from her face. Steve and I managed to cut our phone line, cable, and electric dog fence, and our one-day project turned into four. But we got it done, and that sprinkler system is the gift that keeps on giving. Every time the little sprinklers pop up out of our yard, Laurie gets a little jolt of joy that even causes her to feel romantic toward me. I never should have waited fifteen years. I even sneak out of the house sometimes to turn it on just to see what might happen. Start investing in the people who are closest to you, beginning with your wife and family.

Stop Looking for Perfect People

Second, you need to stop looking for perfect people because they don't exist. I never put it into words, but somewhere in the back of my mind I kept thinking that somewhere out there was the perfect set of friends who would always gel with me: people who were confident but humble; conversant but quiet; strong but gentle; happy but not over the top; creative but not weird; and spiritual but not religious. In addition, they would be athletic, competitive, balanced, fun, and able to talk sports and theology in the same breath. These people don't exist. Every human being has at least one quirk, habit, or flaw that drives other people batty.

I remember the exact moment when I looked around the table during our leadership team meeting and said to myself, "Why am I looking for anyone else? These people are not perfect, but they're about as good as it gets." I knew that every one of our leadership team members has flaws. And they could point out my flaws. What's more, there are times when each one of them really gets on my nerves, and I really get on their nerves. We've had our moments, and we'll continue to have moments. That's because no matter how spiritually mature each of us is, we're still sinners who occasionally say and do things that irritate each other. We all have a dark side that needs to be constantly managed and forgiven.

But I made a conscious decision in that moment that these are the people with whom I want to do life. These are the ones whom, for whatever reason, God has placed in my life and with whom I want to share life. And that single decision has brought more joy and goodwill to my daily relationships than anything else.

Whom has God placed in your life, and what's preventing you from investing in them? If you have an expectation for perfection that is causing you to withhold your friendship, then it's going to be a long and lonely life.

Bring Some Energy to It

Every relationship takes energy to sustain and feed it. That's why you can't have more than a few friendships that go long and deep. At some point you have to draw a line and say, "I'd like to have a friendship with that person, but if I start sharing life with him or her, that means I have to limit or stop sharing life with someone else." Each of us has a finite amount of time, which means you have to put a limit on the number of people with whom you wish to go long and deep.

And when you share a friendship with someone, you need to bring energy to it; you need to bring some life and joy to it. As I mentioned earlier, for a long season in my life I wasn't doing my part to add life and joy to others. I took far more than I gave. And when you take more than you give, people look for ways to pull away from you.

What I've learned is that being energetic and joyful is often a choice. You can either choose to be energetic and joyful, or you can choose to be a lifeless slug.

I was lying on the couch one day when my son, who was seven years old at the time, came up to me and asked me to play ball with him. My immediate response was, "Dave, I'm tired." I said it without thinking because that was my habit. I'll never forget what happened. He dropped his head, walked away, and said "You're *always* tired." Now that boy is grown and gone, and we're separated by ten states and thirteen hundred miles. I would give anything to have that day back and be able to throw pitches to David. I'd love to pick him up and feel his suntanned arms around my neck, to kiss his check and have him kiss mine back. Those days are long gone. But that day I made a choice to change my words and bring some energy to my son no matter how tired I felt. I began to see that I could actually talk myself into being more energetic and joyful.

What's your most common response when someone asks how you are? Is it "I'm good; I'm great; I'm ready to go," or is it "I'm tired; I'm stressed; I'm in a rotten mood"? Maybe you are tired, stressed, or in a lousy mood, but nobody wants to be around that. Have your pity party and then snap out of it. Bring some energy and joy to the table, and you'll be amazed how that will affect you and those around you. It's a choice!

The Old Testament prophet Habakkuk was at the end of his rope. He was tired and beaten down by ruthless men who were inflicting violence and wickedness on him and his people, so he poured out his woes to God.

> The trees have no blossoms,
> The vines have no grapes,

The olive crop has failed,
The fields are barren,
The flocks are gone,
And the cattle are dead. (Hab. 3:17 paraphrased)

You talk about a bad day; everything around him had either failed or died. But then at the end of the prayer, he said this:

I will rejoice in the LORD!
I will be joyful in the God of my salvation!
The Sovereign LORD is my strength! (Hab. 3:18–19 NLT)

Habakkuk made a choice that, while pain and loss are inevitable, misery is optional. Some of us need to make a choice that in spite of our disappointments, we can still be joyful by trusting in God's sovereign plan. It really is a choice.

There's a father of three energetic teenage boys in our church, and every time I ask Scott how he's doing he says, "It's always a sunny day in my life." I can assure you that Scott has just as many pressures and disappointments as anyone else, but he has made a choice not to let those things define him. And every time he says, "It's always a sunny day in my life," I smile. Just hearing those words makes me a little happier. Bring some energy to your relationships.

Limit Your Time with Drainers and Downers

Relational integrity is a two-way street. If you're trying to relate to someone with honesty, kindness, and generosity, but they have no interest in returning the same to you, then by definition it's not a relationship. Life is too short to spend it with drainers and downers. If you're not experiencing much joy in life, check your relationships, because people can either enhance your life or put a damper on it.

Proverbs 15:30 says, "A friendly smile makes you happy" (CEV). Psalm 133:1 says, "How good and pleasant it is when brothers live together in unity!" Do certain people make something inside you light up when you see them? It could be your spouse, a relative, hopefully a friend or two. I urge you to spend more of your time with those people and less of your time with people who are what Erwin McManus calls "emotional leeches." These are the people who suck the life out of you because no matter how much you pour into them, they just take and take and never give back.

The hard truth is that there are people in your world and mine who are somewhat toxic. No matter how much love and attention you give them, they refuse to take responsibility for their lives and instead blame you for all their problems. So they say things like, "You make me mad," because they think you're responsible for their happiness. Or "You ruined my day," because they think you're responsible for their failures. These people think it's everybody else's fault that they are miserable.

The truth is this: people are responsible for their own life and happiness, not their parents, family, friends, or even their spouse, if they're married. These people can certainly add or subtract from their joy, but ultimately, each person is responsible for his or her own happiness. At some point, joyless, lifeless people need to take responsibility for their life and pursue healing, pursue God, or take medication and get professional help if needed. Only then can they expect to enter into life-giving relationships.

At the same time, we need to love joyless people the best we can; we need to be patient and tolerant as we're able. But we also need to be careful not to allow them to drive or drain our life. We may even need to limit our exposure to them.

Some of you might be thinking, "But what if it's my spouse who is joyless?" Well, they may be joyless because your marriage is joyless. So what are your options?

Have you talked about it? Have you made them aware of your feelings? Don't assume that your spouse knows how you feel, because they might be clueless. Have you read any good books together that can open up a dialogue? Have you done something or gone somewhere lately that brings you both joy? Have you worked on your own relating patterns? Ultimately, the only person you can change is you, and when you improve your own patterns, this can have a positive effect on your spouse's joy.

Have you gone to counseling? I believe that every human being needs to go to counseling at some point in their life because we all have negative stuff that we can't see about ourselves. Everybody else sees it, so why not do yourself and everyone else a big favor and ask a professional to help you? You can't fix things that you can't see or don't know about. There are always options.

Relational integrity is a two-way street, and if you spend your whole life with toxic people, you will become a toxic person. That's not what God intends for you. God said, "How good and pleasant it is when brothers live together in unity!" (Ps. 133:1). So how good and pleasant are the people with whom you spend most of your time?

Practice Forgiveness Every Day

I've been working my way through the book of Matthew, and yesterday I came to chapter 18. At one point Jesus is very direct and says, "If your brother sins against you, go and show him his fault, just between the two of you. If he listens to you, you have won your brother over" (Matt. 18:15). But he says that if this brother won't listen, you should take one or two others with you to confront him again. And if that doesn't work, you should bring the matter before the whole church. And if that doesn't work, then Jesus says, "Treat him as you would a pagan or a tax collector" (v. 17). So Jesus is very direct about confronting sin—this is part of the Christian life.

But a few verses later Peter asks Jesus, "How many times shall I forgive my brother when he sins against me? Up to seven times?" Jesus responds, "Not seven times, but seventy-seven times" (vv. 21–22). In other words, as many times as it takes to restore the relationship. So on the one hand Jesus instructs us to confront the person who sins against us, and on the other hand he instructs us to extend forgiveness as many times as it takes. Truth and grace always go together for Jesus, and both are needed in every healthy relationship.

But what caused me to look up from the chapter and think about my life was Jesus's parable of the unmerciful servant. In this parable, a servant is deeply indebted to his master, who says he's going to throw his servant into prison until he repays all his debts. But when the servant begs for mercy, the master takes pity on him, cancels his debts, and lets him go.

Then this servant goes out and finds a worker who owes him some money. But when the worker begs for mercy, the servant doesn't give it to him. Instead, he throws the worker into prison until he repays all the money.

When the master finds out that his servant did not extend the same mercy to another, he calls him a "wicked servant," throws him into prison, and keeps him there until he repays his debt. Jesus's final words are: "This is how my heavenly Father will treat each of you unless you forgive your brother from your heart" (Matt. 18:35).

How deep is my debt of sin? More than I could ever repay. How much of my debt has the Master forgiven? All of it—cancelled, forgiven, set free. So because the Master has forgiven me, I must forgive all others. I am not given a choice. If I wish to live under the forgiveness and mercy of God, I must extend the same forgiveness and mercy to those who sin against me. I can be honest about and confront their sin for the sake of our relationship, but I can no longer hold a grudge, stay mad, and seek revenge if I wish to live under God's grace. Because I have been forgiven, I must forgive. How many times? Seven times? "No," Jesus says. "You must forgive the same person seventy-seven times," which means every time.

This is a major part of forming a softer soul. I run into someone who irritates me just about every day—a relative, staff member, church person, or some random person who happens to intersect my life. And I can form little grudges in my heart, little battle lines. I may even say something snippy or withhold a kind gesture to punish that person. But when I do, my heart gets a little harder, and I lose the chance to experience the goodness in that person. Jesus said we must extend forgiveness seventy-seven times, with our spouse, kids, neighbors, co-workers, random people who annoy us. Little forgivenesses all day long, "from your heart," Jesus says, is the key to a relationally rich life.

> Because the Master has forgiven me, I must forgive all others.

Shauna Niequist writes about her battle with forgiveness in her book *Cold Tangerines*. She likens it to keeping someone on the "hook."

When I'm trying to forgive someone I picture myself physically lifting that person off a big hook. I never want to. I prefer to stew and focus my anger on them like a laser pointer. . . . I hope that they will get fat and people will talk about them behind their backs and their toilets will overflow and their computers crash. Earlier this year, a friend of mine made me really mad. Crazy mad. . . . For a while, it brought me so much joy to be angry with her and to put her back up on the hook, over and over. . . . And I wanted her to apologize for what she did. Loudly. Publically. And give me a present too. . . . But nothing. No phone calls. No emails. No large, fragrant bouquets of flowers. Nothing. Why should I forgive someone who doesn't even think she needs to be forgiven? This is why. Because I want my neck and my back muscles to stop hurting. Because I want to sleep instead of having endless imaginary conversations. Because I want my mind back. Because I want my life back. Because she's not the only one on the hook. Because every time I hang her up on that hook, the hook reaches down and grabs me, too.[2]

Peter asked Jesus how many times he should forgive someone, and Jesus told him as many times as it takes. Partly because when you and I let others off the hook, we let ourselves
off the hook.

Niequist concludes:

> So I let her off the hook. I let her off once, until someone
> brought her name up at lunch, and then I got mad all over
> again, which threw me for a loop. I *forgave* her. Why am I still
> so mad at her? I realized I had to take her off the hook every
> single time, not just one big time. I had to take her off the
> hook in the morning, and then again at lunch. . . . Over and
> over, all day, I had to keep letting her off the hook, because
> when I do, I can breathe again.[3]

Forgiveness is one of the hardest things to do, and it doesn't
mean you have to forget what the person did to you. Forgetting
can help free you from the painful memory, but sometimes
it's not possible to forget, at least not right away. You might
not be able to forget for a long time, maybe never, but you
can still choose to forgive and let it go—for *your* sake.

Forgiveness also doesn't mean you have to be friends with
that person. It doesn't mean you have to spend time with or
begin trusting that person. Those things are earned. Some
people haven't earned the right to be trusted. You may need
to create some specific boundaries between you and them
until they've proven they can be trusted.

Love gets tested the most when someone crosses you or of-
fends you. Jesus says that it's easy to love those who love you;
anybody can do that. The real test of love, the real show of
forgiveness is when you choose to let someone off the hook,
even when they've wronged you.

Stop Waiting to Start Loving

It's easy to breeze past people and take them for granted—
especially the ones closest to you. It's taken me a long time

to realize that the people God has put into my life every day at home and at work are the people God wants me to love. And the truth is that this is the only day you and I have to love. We don't have tomorrow promised to us. So don't wait. Don't let the words *maybe* and *someday* determine your life and love. Make plans, send the email, arrange the lunch, spend some money, book the flight.

Several years ago an article appeared in the *Los Angeles Times*. A lady named Ann Wells wrote words that have never left me:

> My brother-in-law opened the bottom drawer of my sister's bureau and lifted out a tissue-wrapped package. "This," he said, "is not a slip. This is lingerie." He discarded the tissue and handed me the slip. It was exquisite: silk and trimmed with a cobweb of lace. The price tag was still attached.
>
> Jan bought this the first time we went to New York, at least eight or nine years ago. She never wore it. She was saving it for a special occasion. Well, I guess this is the occasion.
>
> He took the slip from me and put it on the bed with the other clothes we were taking to the mortician. His hands lingered on the soft material for a moment, then he slammed the drawer shut and turned to me.
>
> "Don't ever save anything for a special occasion. Every day you're alive is a special occasion."
>
> I remembered those words through the funeral and the days that followed when I helped him attend to all the sad chores that follow an unexpected death. I thought about them on the plane returning to California from the Midwestern town where my sister's family lives. I thought about all the things that she hadn't seen or heard or done. I thought about the things she had done without realizing they were special.
>
> I'm still thinking about his words, and they've changed my life. I'm not "saving" anything; we use our good china and crystal for every special event—such as losing a pound or getting the sink unstopped.
>
> "Someday" and "one of these days" are losing their grip on my vocabulary. If it's worth seeing or hearing or doing,

I want to see and hear and do it now. I'm trying very hard not to put off, hold back, or save anything that would add laughter and luster to our lives.

And every morning when I open my eyes I tell myself that it is special.[4]

We all live frantic lives filled with work, commuting, exercising, grocery shopping, bill paying, and unexpected crises—nobody is exempt. But I hope you can begin to see that every day God gives is special and that we need to stop waiting to start loving. After all, life comes down to the people in it. Every single day is a gift. Every single day you and I are faced with the choice to love. Jesus said, "And this is my command, that you love one another." Not tomorrow, not next year but today—this day.

C. S. Lewis wrote wise words regarding this choice:

> Every time you make a choice you turn into something a little different than you were before. And taking your life as a whole, with all your innumerable choices, all your life long you are slowly turning either into a heavenly creature or into a hellish creature; either into a creature that is in harmony with God and others, or into someone who is in a state of war with God and others. To be one kind of creature is joy, peace and power. To be the other means madness, rage and eternal loneliness. Each of us at each moment is progressing to the one state or the other.[5]

A few months ago I was walking through O'Hare airport with a pastor friend from Minneapolis. I'm fifty-three, and Jerry is sixty-three. So I said, "Jerry, you're ten years older than me. What advice would you give me for my next ten years?"

Without hesitation he looked at me and said, "Enjoy it." He went on to say that the last decade of his life flew by—like it was just a month. He said that he failed to enjoy it like he should have.

I've thought about his words many times, and I think he's right—barring any tragedy or premature death, sixty-three is going to come in my life, and if it's anything like the last ten years, it's going to come sometime next week.

What will the next ten years be like for you? Will you express daily love to those God has brought into your life? Will you forgive others as Jesus has forgiven you? And will you try to see the joy in every day God gives you?

The choice to become more of a heavenly creature than a hellish one is available to each of us. And with God's help, we will make the right choice—for our sake and for God's glory.

The choice to become more of a heavenly creature than a hellish one is available to each of us. And with God's help, we will make the right choice—for our sake and for God's glory.

Bob Merritt has been the senior pastor of Eagle Brook Church, outside St. Paul, MN, since 1991, leading the church through a period of explosive growth. In his messages, he tackles tough topics and answers life-changing questions about faith, family, and much more—while keeping the church's mission to reach others for Christ at the forefront. He holds an MA in divinity from Bethel Seminary and a PhD in speech communications from Pennsylvania State University. Bob and his wife, Laurie, live in White Bear Lake and have two adult children. Bob does not tweet.

Visit Bob Merritt at bobmerritt.net.

Notes

Chapter 1

1. M. Scott Peck, MD, *The Road Less Traveled: A New Psychology of Love, Traditional Values, and Spiritual Growth* (New York: Simon & Schuster, 1978), 15.

2. Ibid.

3. Judy White Edelson, "Not All Bridges Can Be Burned," *Newsweek*, December 13, 1993, 8.

4. Bill Hybels, *Who You Are (When No One's Looking)* (Downers Grove, IL: InterVarsity, 1987), 29.

5. Henry Cloud, *Integrity: The Courage to Meet the Demands of Reality* (New York: HarperCollins, 2006), 200.

Chapter 2

1. "Girl, Guide Drown in BWCA: 17-year-old Church Camper from Iowa Pulled Under, 24-year-old Man Dies Trying to Save Her," *St. Paul Pioneer Press*, August 1, 2002.

2. C. S. Lewis, quoted in Charles Colson, *The Good Life: Seeking Purpose, Meaning, and Truth in Your Life* (Carol Stream, IL: Tyndale, 2005), 120.

3. Scott Waddle, *The Right Thing* (Nashville: Thomas Nelson, 2003), 234.

Chapter 3

1. Bill Hybels, *Who You Are (When No One's Looking)* (Downers Grove, IL: InterVarsity, 1987), 47.

Chapter 4

1. Max Lucado, *A Gentle Thunder: Hearing God through the Storm* (Dallas: Word, 1995), 30.

2. Kerry Shook and Chris Shook, *One Month to Live: Thirty Days to a No-Regrets Life* (Colorado Springs: WaterBrook, 2008), 13.

3. Andy Stanley, *The Next Generation Leader: Five Essentials for Those Who Will Shape the Future* (Sisters, OR: Multnomah, 2003), 29.

4. Lance Armstrong, *It's Not about the Bike: My Journey Back to Life* (New York: Berkley Books, 2000), 191, 194.

5. Ibid., 218–20.

6. Shook and Shook, *One Month to Live*, 16.

7. Jim Collins, *Good to Great: Why Some Companies Make the Leap . . . and Others Don't* (New York: Harper-Collins, 2001), 139.

8. Lloyd Reeb, *From Success to Significance: When the Pursuit of Success Isn't Enough* (Grand Rapids: Zondervan, 2004), 105.

9. Max Lucado, *Cure for the Common Life: Living in Your Sweet Spot* (Nashville: Thomas Nelson, 2005), 148.

10. Marcus Buckingham, *Go Put Your Strengths to Work* (New York: Free Press, 2007), 89.

Chapter 5

1. Sam Walton and John Huey, *Sam Walton: Made in America* (New York: Doubleday, 1992), 35.

2. Oren Dorell, "Lottery Winners' Good Luck Can Go Bad Fast," *USA Today*, February 26, 2006.

3. Andy Stanley, *The Principle of the Path: How to Get from Where You Are to Where You Want to Be* (Nashville: Thomas Nelson, 2008), 14.

4. Ibid., 55.

5. Henry Cloud, *Nine Things You Simply Must Do to Succeed in Love and Life: A Psychologist Learns from His Patients What Works and What Doesn't* (Brentwood, TN: Integrity, 2004), 74.

Chapter 6

1. Travis Bradberry and Jean Greaves, *Emotional Intelligence 2.0* (San Diego: TalentSmart, 2009), 7.

2. Jim Collins, *Good to Great: Why Some Companies Make the Leap . . . and Others Don't* (New York: Harper-Collins, 2001), 127.

3. Jim Citrin, "Tapping the Power of Your Morning Routine," www.finance. yahoo.com, January 30, 2007.

4. Lisa Rogak, *Haunted Heart: The Life and Times of Stephen King* (New York: Thomas Dunne Books, 2009), 93.

5. "An Interview with John Grisham," *San Francisco Chronicle*, February 5, 2008.

6. C. S. Lewis, *Surprised by Joy* (New York: Harvest Books, 1955), 136.

7. Phillip C. McGraw, *Family First: Your Step-by-Step Plan for Creating a Phenomenal Family* (New York: Free Press, 2004), 43.

8. Ibid., 48.

9. Dr. Ron Jenson, *Make a Life, Not Just a Living: Ten Timeless Life Skills That Will Maximize Your Real Net Worth* (Nashville: Thomas Nelson, 1995), 11.

Chapter 7

1. Human Performance Institute, "Energy for Performance Course," workbook, 2007, 14.

2. John M. Gottman, PhD, and Joan DeClaire, *The Relationship Cure: A Five-Step Guide to Strengthening Your Marriage, Family, and Friendships* (New York: Three Rivers Press, 2001), 4.

3. Ibid.

4. Matthew E. May, *The Elegant Solution: Toyota's Formula for Mastering Innovation* (New York: Free Press, 2007), 43.

5. Ibid., 49.

6. Jennifer Silvera, *Believe: A Young Widow's Journey through Brokenness and Back* (Grand Rapids: Kregel, 2009), 52.

7. Ibid., 81.

8. Ibid., 27.

9. Ibid., 60.

10. Ibid., 105.

11. Ibid., 110.

12. Ibid., 110, 114, 120.

Chapter 8

1. Henry Cloud, *Integrity: The Courage to Meet the Demands of Reality* (New York: HarperCollins, 2006), 229.

2. Ibid.

3. Ibid., 230.

4. Erwin Raphael McManus, *Seizing Your Divine Moment: Dare to Live a Life of Adventure* (Nashville: Thomas Nelson, 2002), 147.

5. Cloud, *Integrity*, 211.

Chapter 9

1. Leanne Italie, "Divorce Lawyers: Facebook Tops in Online Evidence," www.news.yahoo.com, June 28, 2010.

2. Wayne Cordeiro, *The Divine Mentor: Growing Your Faith as You Sit at the Feet of the Savior* (Bloomington, MN: Bethany, 2007), 59.

3. Erwin Raphael McManus, *Seizing Your Divine Moment: Dare to Live a Life of Adventure* (Nashville: Thomas Nelson, 2002), 22.

Chapter 10

1. Lynne and Bill Hybels, *Rediscovering Church: The Story and Vision of Willow Creek Community Church* (Grand Rapids: Zondervan, 1995), 108.

2. Marcus Buckingham and Curt Coffman, *First, Break All the Rules: What the World's Greatest Ma[nagers] Do Differently* (New York: Sim[on and] Schuster, 1999), 79.

3. Dan Pierson, "Holmgren[...] to NFL's Top QBs," *Chicago Tr[ibune]*, December 26, 1996.

Chapter 11

1. James MacDonald, *I Really [Want] to Change . . . so Help Me God* [(Chi]cago: Moody, 2000), 26.

2. Larry Crabb, "The Sure R[oute] to Madness," *Conversations: A Fo[rum] for Authentic Transformation* 1 (Sp[ring] 2003): 10.

3. MacDonald, *I Really Wan[t to] Change*, 63.

Chapter 12

1. Gary Chapman, *The Five L[ove] Languages: How to Express Heart[felt] Commitment to Your Mate* (Chica[go:] Northfield, 1992), 15.

2. Shauna Niequist, *Cold Tang[er]ines: Celebrating the Extraordinary N[a]ture of Everyday Life* (Grand Rapi[ds:] Zondervan, 2007), 165, 167.

3. Ibid., 168.

4. Ann Wells, "What Special Som[e]day Are We Saving For?" *Los Angel[es] Times*, April 14, 1985.

5. C. S. Lewis, *Mere Christiani[ty]* (New York: Macmillian, 1952), 87.